FOR THE LOVE OF COD

Also by Eric Dregni
Published by the University of Minnesota Press

In Cod We Trust: Living the Norwegian Dream

Vikings in the Attic: In Search of Nordic America

*Never Trust a Thin Cook and Other Lessons from
Italy's Culinary Capital*

Let's Go Fishing! Fish Tales from the North Woods

By the Waters of Lake Minnetonka

You're Sending Me Where? Dispatches from Summer Camp

Minnesota Marvels: Roadside Attractions in the Land of Lakes

*Midwest Marvels: Roadside Attractions across Iowa,
Minnesota, the Dakotas, and Wisconsin*

FOR THE LOVE OF COD

A Father and Son's Search
for Norwegian Happiness

ERIC DREGNI

UNIVERSITY OF MINNESOTA PRESS
MINNEAPOLIS
LONDON

Published by the University of Minnesota Press
111 Third Avenue South, Suite 290
Minneapolis, MN 55401-2520
http://www.upress.umn.edu

ISBN 978-1-5179-0893-5 (hc/j)

Library of Congress record available at https://lccn.loc.gov/2020058652

Printed in the United States of America on acid-free paper

The University of Minnesota is an equal-opportunity educator and employer.

26 25 24 23 22 21   10 9 8 7 6 5 4 3 2 1

Contents

Lykkelig

Happy-Go-Lucky

MY DAD TOOK ME TO SCANDINAVIA when I was sixteen. Now it was my turn to take my son. The only problem was I didn't have the money.

Thirty-five years after my dad brought me back to "the homeland," I realized he had given me the gift of a true view of the origin of our ancestors and the struggles they went through to cross the ocean. The vague images I had of Scandinavia, which were based largely on stereotypes, things I'd read and watched, and family lore, were put to the test as we traveled together by train and bicycle to visit relatives and take in the stunning scenery illuminated with gentle summer sun. Although I could embrace or reject parts of this Scandinavian background, I could no longer ignore that this was part of my identity.

Now I wanted my son Eilif to have the same revelation. If he were just exposed to the complexities of these forward-looking countries that are steeped in history, perhaps his world would be opened up too. Eilif had spent five summers at a Norwegian language camp in northern Minnesota, so I imagined he'd be ready for a big voyage over to the homeland.

The only problem was I didn't have the money. I looked at our finances and saw that we couldn't afford two airline tickets. To cut expenses, I figured out a way to co-lead a trip around Norway to pay for my ticket. I'd stay there afterward, and Eilif could fly over to meet me.

In planning our trip, I discovered we couldn't afford to stay in hotels either. I'd already told Eilif about this grand plan, however, so I hesitated canceling his ticket. I wrote to friends and relatives in Norway, begging them to let us sleep in their spare bedrooms for a couple of nights.

Norway is no longer the most expensive country in the world (as of this writing, it's moved to fourth place), but it can now boast that it's the "happiest country in the world," according to the World Happiness Report from the United Nations in 2017. I was perplexed. My wife, Katy, and I had lived in Trondheim for a year, and it had never struck me as a glowingly joyous place, with its dark winters and reserved citizens. "What does 'happiness' even mean?" a tour guide in Stockholm had once asked me, with perhaps a bit of envy. "I don't see the Norwegians as any happier than us Swedes."

Eilif's godmother, Inger, in Oslo also didn't understand this new rating. "Happiness? We have bad weather, the highest prices for beer, and things are so expensive!"

When my dad had taken me to Scandinavia for a few weeks when I was a teenager, I remember easily affording flashy New Wave clothes in Oslo (the Norwegian band A-ha was at the top of the charts at the time). I was enamored with the laid-back but stylish lifestyle and the way people started sentences with "*We* believe that . . ." or "*We* like . . ." I'd never heard that before since I would never assume I knew what other people believe or like. They seemed to speak this way to show unity and a sense of community.

Perhaps this is why Eilif had also latched on to his Nordic roots? "I'm Norwegian," he declared, but I wonder if it's true.

Eilif was born near Trondheim fifteen years ago, but the Norwegian government didn't automatically give him citizenship. Technically he was without any citizenship for his first few weeks of life as we waited for the U.S. Embassy in Oslo to approve his passport. Perhaps what it means to be Norwegian—or American for that matter—is an open question, but I can't say he's wrong to want to claim this other nationality.

His first name, Eilif, is very Norwegian, but he only lived in Norway for his first seven months. Our last name, originally Drægni, is from the Sognefjord, but I'm only one-eighth Norwegian. How "Norwegian" can we be? Katy thanks her stars that she isn't Scandinavian and was able to avoid that particular superiority complex, after marrying me and dealing with a family that is a little too proud.

She gave birth to Eilif outside of Trondheim the year we lived there. The Norwegian government paid for the delivery, plus gave us a bonus five thousand dollars to help with expenses. Could all of this financial help be one of the reasons for Norwegian happiness?

The Norwegians knocked the Danes out of first place in the happiness battle in 2017, and then the Finns were crowned as the kings of cheer the year after. Really? My friend Emily who went to teach in Copenhagen asked her third grade Danish students why Norway got this year's prize. "They only got it because they have so much money," little Buster complained, and his classmates enthusiastically agreed. They assured their teacher that Denmark is still better.

A former honorary consul of Denmark once told me, "The Danes are so happy because they have low expectations. If you don't expect anything good to happen, everything is fine. I wake up thinking that I could be dead. If I'm alive, then I'm happy." Hardly a glowing outlook on life.

Perhaps this reflects the clichéd Minnesotan saying, "It could be worse." As in, during subzero winters when everything is terrible, at least you haven't lost a limb to frostbite (yet). If this is the scale of happiness, anything looks good. This is vastly different from when Katy and I lived in Italy for a couple of years and people had high expectations of a good life, delicious food, and cool sunglasses. And they complained often.

I found during our time in Norway that Norwegians rarely grumbled about their situation, but they almost never exclaimed about how good they had it either. Though we lived there for one year and I studied the language for almost three, I never learned the exact Norwegian word for "happy." Was this because it's bad form for Norwegians to brag about their good fortune? No one actually told me they were happy—perhaps they didn't want to brag.

Gladelig is more "gladly" than "happy." Too much has been made out of the Danish word *hygge,* which actually comes from Old Norse and means to get cozy and snug. Norwegians also use *landlig,* which is more like country cozy. *Trivelig,* or thriving, is perhaps the best translation. Eilif's godfather and Inger's husband, Knut, suggested *"lykkelig,* which defines those precious moments when everything comes together."

I then noticed this word in many places. A cheesy feel-good poster in a hotel in Vågåmo declared, *"Lykkelig ar den som har lidenskap,"* or "Happy are those who have passion."

Many wish me *"Lykke til!,"* which means "good luck" but looks like "happiness to you." Besides, I thought that *heldig* meant "lucky." I had once asked Petter Hovin, a bus driver from Trondheim, about it, who explained, "When you bet and win, you are *heldig*, but when you are *lykkelig* you make your own luck. You set the stage for your happiness and don't necessarily rely just on fortune for your happiness."

Perhaps this sums up the Norwegian mentality that the country has worked hard to achieve its goals and deserves happiness. Many neighboring Scandinavians think Norwegians just got lucky by striking oil in the North Sea. In other words, they were lucky when "happiness was handed to them on a platter," or *når lykken kommer rekende på en fjøl*. On my trip with Eilif, I wanted to learn more Norwegian words and expressions, beyond *hygge* and other corny phrases that get turned into tea towels. Maybe I lost something in translation during our year there, or perhaps the famous Scandinavian stoicism prevented me from understanding Norwegians' overall satisfaction with their system. I originally wrote about my family's experiences in Trondheim in the book *In Cod We Trust*, but the country seems to have changed since then. Now that Norway is officially one of the happiest places on earth, whatever that means, I had to investigate. Only a return trip to the country where Eilif was born could answer my questions. I want our kids to be as happy as possible, of course, and Eilif was thinking about his next steps now that he had completed his first year of high school. Perhaps the Norwegians could give us some tips.

I also wanted to see if Eilif could ever fit in there as a student—or if that would even be a good idea. Should he pursue a free university degree at the glorious Gløshaugen campus in Trondheim with its Harry Potter-esque gothic styling? Then I remembered the hazing ritual for their botany students: their faces painted green and marched through town in green pajamas with green Dahl's beer cases on their heads. Oh, and the students who ate raw fish innards and crawled into barrels that stored fish to prove that they were worthy of the marine biology department. Hmm, our son would probably love these college shenanigans.

My Norwegian friend Tor approved of Eilif's plan to go to Norway: "Of course he wants to find a good Norwegian girl," as if that's every boy's dream. When I told this to Katy, who has a solid Irish background, she laughed that of course our side of the family considers "Norwegian" to be synonymous with "perfect."

I'm not thrilled with the idea of Eilif settling down overseas, but I did wonder what secrets of a happy life he and I could learn from this northern country of just five million people, fewer even than our home state of Minnesota. I read any books and articles I could get my hands on related to Norwegian happiness, but I wanted to hear directly from Norwegians if they really are so happy—and to find out if there's another, darker side to Norway that no one wants to complain about. And by staying with friends and relatives, I could surreptitiously interview our hosts over strong coffee and learn their secrets of a supposedly blissful life.

That year, Eilif's school would be letting out several weeks before his two younger siblings were set free, and Katy worried, "I don't want him bouncing around the house!" Another incentive to send him abroad with me. And so Katy stayed home this time and instead sent Eilif over to visit his birthplace and to get him out of her hair.

I would leave for Norway a couple of weeks before Eilif, to co-lead a group of travelers who would head home around the time Eilif arrived. I'd be over my jet lag by then and ready for Eilif's energy and his constant music—he insisted on bringing his acoustic guitar. I just had to remind myself that I had been equally obsessed with music when my dad took me around Scandinavia.

Once Eilif arrived in Bergen, we would spend a couple of nights with Inger's brother and then board the coastal steamer for a two-day passage up to Trondheim to see his birthplace. From there, we'd hop on the train for a ten-hour trip to visit relatives north of the Arctic Circle. Finally, we'd fly down to the capital of Oslo for a few days in the big city.

As Katy prepared to put Eilif on the international flight from Minneapolis to Bergen, a KLM representative told her that she could pay an extra fee to have them watch over our "unaccompanied minor."

"You mean, like a babysitter?" Eilif gasped.

The representative told her that it was indeed mostly for young kids, who are brought to a special kids' area in the airport.

"Like day care? In a play area? Obviously, you don't trust me."

The representative confided, "Actually, if he's responsible, you probably don't need it."

Eilif insisted, "I'll be fine on my own!"

Katy nervously went over with Eilif how to transfer planes in the Amsterdam airport. She'd drop him off in Minneapolis and I'd pick him up on the other end.

What could go wrong?

Adult Points

EILIF'S PLANE WAS CIRCLING high above my head in Bergen when I got the news. "We're going to Warsaw," he texted.

I immediately went over to the KLM desk to ask why the plane wasn't landing and to get some clarification on this bizarre message.

The KLM representative scrambled around, consulted her computer. "We have no idea what's going on with that plane," she said.

Not good.

"Are you serious?" I asked. "Don't you have any contact with the plane? Why would the plane be going to Warsaw?"

She had no answers, which of course made me conclude that the plane had been hijacked with our fifteen-year-old unaccompanied minor aboard. He'd been taken hostage by Polish terrorists—if there even was such a thing. It didn't help that Eilif had stopped responding to texts (as I found out later, his phone's battery was nearly dead). He wasn't supposed to be using it on the plane anyway.

Despite the seven-hour time difference, Katy called from Minneapolis, and we desperately tried to figure out what was going on. Finally, Eilif texted that he had mis-heard the Dutch, Norwegian, and German announcements over the intercom and that the plane was going to *Oslo*, not *Warsaw*. The KLM representative confirmed this and added that the plane was having problems with its landing gear in one of the wings and needed a longer runway. Somehow this didn't calm our fears.

Eilif had navigated through the Amsterdam airport flawlessly, but now the airline was sending him alone to the wrong city, more than six hours away by train. By the time we figured all this out, the plane was about to land in Oslo. What would he do there? Would they send him back to Bergen?

I called the KLM desk in Oslo to see if they could help him. "All the passengers are now off the plane," the representative said happily.

"Wait! Did you see our fifteen-year-old son? Is he gone?"

"Just call him. He can come up to the help desk, and either we'll get him on the next flight to Bergen or we'll get him a hotel for the night and a flight out the next day."

"His phone is dead," I explained, trying to remain calm, "and he has no idea what to do. You need to find him!"

Katy called and we remembered that Eilif's godparents, Knut and Inger, live in Oslo. They saved the day by agreeing to pick him up at the airport (if they could find him). Eilif finally managed to charge his phone and said he was waiting at Peppes Pizza in the airport. We told him not to move and that Knut would find him, somehow, even if he hadn't seen Eilif for almost a decade.

We waited impatiently for news.

Inger called an hour later with the news that Eilif was safe with them and had eaten enough for three adults. He was resting on the couch. "He earned his *voksenpoeng* for this adventure. He was a pro!" She explained that *voksenpoeng* are "grow points" or "adult points" that kids earn in Norway when they are extra responsible. Eilif was terribly proud of this. I didn't dare say that it reminded me of the potty charts we used to tape up in the bathroom when he was a toddler and the Lightning McQueen sticker we placed on the chart each time he used the big-boy toilet. I was just happy that he wasn't in the dungeon of some Polish terrorist.

Knut and Inger assured us that Norway is safe. A couple of years ago they let their thirteen-year-old daughter, Ada, travel alone around the busy city of Oslo on the trams, buses, and even ferries to visit friends on the other side of town and on the islands. "I have to be willing to let other people take part in my daughter's upbringing," Inger explained. "Norwegian kids have good relations with their parents. We're not too authoritarian and don't give orders." This fits into the Norwegian idea of a *fri oppdragelse,* or "free upbringing," referring to the theory that children shouldn't be held back or scolded.

At the time, I was staying with Inger's brother Jan in Bergen, who agreed that kids roaming around in Norway is perfectly normal. His ten-year-old son Alexander takes a taxi to school since there's no bus. Jan's wife, Tonja, added, "Our daughter Aurora has to take the tram and city bus, so she started at ten years old."

"At ten? Really?" I ask.

"Yes, together we went through how to do it," Jan explained. "In Norway, it is suggested that you don't let kids go alone until ten. It's not a law, but it's a good idea." I remembered being in Bergen a couple of years before for *syttende mai,* or Norwegian Constitution Day, and seeing young kids gathered with no apparent supervision. Jarle, a teacher from Oslo, had once said to me, "Kids are free to roam. There are no body snatchers here!"

That said, the specter of the terrible homegrown terrorist attack in 2011 that killed seventy-seven people, mostly kids, looms over the country. Torstein, a Swedish German bus driver I'd met who works in Norway, told me, "Nothing changed after that terrorist attack, whereas in Stockholm and Frankfurt it's all militarized." I did notice for the first time during that same trip that a policeman in a flak jacket with a submachine gun guarded one of the entrances to Bergen's *syttende mai* parade route. Even so, the Bergen area, with more than four hundred thousand people, has only one to three homicides a year.

Norway is remarkably safe, but Jarle worries that the *fri oppdragelse* is disappearing as mothers and fathers try to enroll kids in too many activities and supervise them too much. "Parents now are so worried that kids are going to hurt themselves, but the parents are often the danger. They are exceeding the speed limits around the schools just to get the kids to their activities and they are caught by police radar."

Just as I've witnessed parenting changes in the United States, I saw increased attention on, or perhaps worry for, kids in Norway too. Now that her daughter Ada was fifteen, Inger wanted to create more rules rather than just treat her as an adult. She liked the Afghan parents at Ada's school, who set up curfews for their kids and were more involved with rules.

I spoke with twenty-four-year-old Stine from Geilo, who said that Norwegian parents are rather strict: "We have a lot of rules, which is really good." When I asked her to give an example, though, all she could think of was, "We can't drink before we're eighteen."

As Eilif was getting older, we were slowly giving him more freedom and even paying for him to go on school trips overseas. Inger said, "We don't have so many exotic trips as they do in Italy or the United States since we have this idea that school should be free and not everyone can afford these trips."

I didn't feel so bad once I heard that Inger and Knut took Ada on lots of trips around Europe, and they had also visited us in Minnesota. With what little money Katy and I had, we spent it on experiences for our kids. Stine from Geilo told me that kids' happiness in Norway was not all about the money. "No! It's that we're equal and no one has so much more money than someone else. We're lucky our parents have money to go on trips, so we aren't sitting around doing nothing."

With these thoughts going through my mind, I picked up Eilif the next morning at the Bergen airport and didn't feel so guilty for spoiling him with this trip. After all, he had earned his *voksenpoeng*.

Seal Clubbing and Whaleburgers

"BERGEN IS ESSENTIALLY ON THE EDGE of the inhabitable world," Jan told us. "Can you live much north of here?"

Bergen in May is a lush rain forest, with the sweet smell of rhododendrons and azaleas in full bloom due to an average rainfall of 80 inches a year. Turbulent weather from the North Sea can't make it over the mountains surrounding the city, so the clouds unleash their load on Bergen. The clouds then rise but get stuck on mountain peaks, so the sun often doesn't shine until it rises above the clouds. This hardly seemed to be the edge of the world, even though we were north of the 60th parallel.

I'd never met Jan before, only his sister Inger, but he graciously agreed to put Eilif and me up in his Bergen home for a few days before we caught the coastal steamer north to Trondheim. He took his hosting responsibilities seriously and even took a break from his part-time job as a local political organizer to take us sightseeing downtown with his wife, Tonja.

We wandered around the Bryggen, or wharf, a UNESCO World Heritage site of four-story wooden buildings and little wooden alleyways where the Germans formerly traded beer for fish. Now they just bring Euros to trade for fish and beer. Bergen is a proud city with a funny accent, as they say there. They also say it's officially the rainiest city on earth—they once had ninety-one straight days of rain, and then one day of clear weather broke the streak. The next day began another solid month of rain.

They call it a city of umbrellas, where people grow webbing between their toes and fingers. We saw umbrella shops and umbrella repairmen. Pages of books leaf open with the humidity, and clothes (especially wool) have that familiar musty smell. If you don't go out in the rain, you'd never go out. I'd seen kids playing in the rain and lining up for school dressed in full rain gear.

Despite the city being constantly wet or in the process of drying out, "90 percent of Bergen has burned down and was built back up again," Kay, a local guide, told me. The giant timber buildings were all rebuilt after a blaze flattened the wharf in 1702. "Each generation has a fire. It either floods or burns." I worry that a fire like the one that happened at the wharf in Stavanger in 2014 could happen to these classic, creaky wooden buildings in Bergen if someone tossed a cigarette butt on a dry wooden board.

I explained to Eilif that his great-great-grandfather Ellef had worked in Bergen as a blacksmith before leaving for Minnesota in 1893. "Why would he leave?" Eilif asked when he looked around at this blossoming city.

I told him that Norway was the poorest country in Europe at the time and that Ellef's hometown at the end of the Lusterfjord had ten times the population it does now and nothing to eat. "Besides, Bergen was famous for lepers and even has a leprosy museum to prove it."

I had also learned from Kay that "the people in Bergen

are called 'the Italians of Norway' because they are direct, gesture with their hands, and have great parties." My great-grandfather had stunning blue eyes and was a "dark" Norwegian with black hair possibly inherited from stray Mediterranean fishermen or, more likely, sailors from the Spanish Armada blown northward in a violent storm. Our family told the tall tale of a Viking forefather falling in love with a Portuguese woman and settling down in the Sognefjord. People in Bergen definitely are more fun loving than most of their fellow countrymen. They even boast that Rome may have seven hills but Bergen has seven mountains.

Each year at the end of May, six to seven thousand people attempt the seven-mountain hike of thirty kilometers up and down each one.

Just like Rome, Bergen always seems festive to me. A couple of days before Eilif arrived, I happened to see Queen Sonja patiently listening to several marching bands as they hailed her, and then she shook all the dignitaries' hands. Afterward, a twenty-one-gun salute of cannons blasted away from the walls of Bergenhus fortress.

Jan and I compared notes about our two countries' political systems, since I was confused that a country as progressive as Norway still has a royal family. In turn, he pointed out that he's appalled at how the United States has taken a reactionary U-turn and horrified the world. Jan is a local representative for the Høyre, or the "Right" party, and described it as the liberal-conservative party. I teased him that this makes no sense in English, since it would be like the "right-left" party.

When Jan had spent time as a student in the United States, he was a young member of the Republican Party, but now he can't recognize the new Republicans and likened them to fascists. Using the terms the Germans used in the 1930s, he listed the steps of how to establish a fascist state and explained how the United States is checking off those boxes one by one. He described how the Republicans' *Gleichschaltung,* or Nazification, uses all the methods for authoritarian control, especially talking about *Lügenpresse,* or the "lying press." Jan used to be a huge proponent of the United States. "I've spent probably a million crowns on private international schools for my kids so they can be more fluent in English than Norwegian—and now the United States is crazy and the Brits chose Brexit."

I in turn told him about how I wrote about Norwegian politics after living in Norway and was dubbed a "mush-headed socialist" spouting "liberal propaganda" and that I should "renounce [my] U.S. citizenship."

I found most Norwegians to be generally pro–United States, but that comes with a big dose of doubt about our intentions, considering our history. I had met a Norwegian man going to Sweden to buy *snus,* or chewing tobacco. When he found out I'm American he wanted to tell me how terrible our government was. "I was in Greenwich Village on September 11, and people were going crazy," he said coolly as if it hadn't really bothered him. "Of course it was terrible, but they ran around saying, 'Why us? What have we done?' As a European, I learned I had to keep my mouth shut or I'd get in trouble telling people why some don't like Americans. I just think it's unforgiveable that they attacked innocent civilians when they could have attacked the White House and the Capitol. I would have applauded if they had killed Bush. They shouldn't hit civilians with the planes, but politicians and the military are legitimate targets."

I had always thought of Norwegians as polite, and I wasn't used to this candor and wondered if this animosity was widespread. I knew that almost all the Norwegian political parties are to the left of the Democrats in the United States, but I didn't expect this. The economist Tor Dahl told me, "One way that Norwegians shine is that I have never heard a politician lie. It's still honorable to be a politician." Then he went on to describe the extremes of the parties. "You have the reds, then the red reds; then you have the blues and the blue blues; then the Christians; then the farmers, populists, environmentalists. There are eight parties that are fluid, and they have to have a coalition. This forces cooperation and sharing of power."

Norwegian political parties don't bad-mouth each other much since they will likely have to form a coalition sometime, but of course there are exceptions. The far-right Progress Party pushed for no immigrants to Norway and ran a notorious candidate, Martin Schanche, a former rallycross driver. During a debate, Schanche slapped the Labour Party candidate Torgeir Micaelsen, who called him a coward live on television.

Another outrageous group, the Kystpartiet, or "Coast Party," has a colorful candidate, Steinar Bastesen, who was proud to be a whale hunter. For his grand entrance to the Norwegian Parliament, the Storting, he dressed in clothes made of sealskin and would regularly eat whaleburgers. I pointed out to friends that whale harpooning and seal clubbing don't go down real well with much of the world. Jan's sister Inger conceded, "Seals are so cute, but there are so many of them." I suppose this is the same way we justify deer hunting in Minnesota.

Despite these examples, everyone I spoke to had a high degree of trust in their government. "I trust in my system," Inger said. "I trust our politicians more than an Italian would, for example." This was an easy comparison, however, since just about every Italian I knew when we lived in Italy didn't trust their government. Even so, I was impressed that just about every Norwegian I met generally thought that their politicians had their hearts in the right place.

A professor of education from Bergen told me, "There's strong confidence in our politicians. We trust them. The basic things are shared by all parties. The most heated discussion was how many wolves to kill."

In the last general election, 78 percent of Norwegians voted. Compare that to the United States, where the turnout of the last general election was 49 percent. Part of the reason, perhaps, is that in Norway even prisoners and ex-convicts can vote. Anna, a law student from Oslo studying at the University of Minnesota, explained that voting is like citizenship, even for felons. "This is their right as human beings. No one can take that away from you since you're born with it."

I asked her whether the terrorist Anders Breivik should be allowed to vote after slaughtering seventy-seven innocent people. "Well, that's not easy," she responded, "but it's strange here to think that you go to jail and suddenly you lose your rights."

Norwegian jails are considered a "prison utopia" because inmates garden, cook, play sports, ski, and sometimes even have music recording studios. The directorate of the Norwegian Correctional Service claims that a jail sentence is a loss of liberty but that inmates retain all other rights. The recidivism rate of criminals in Norway is only 20 percent, whereas in the United States about 76 percent of freed inmates are arrested again within the first five years of release.

Breivik is serving a twenty-one-year sentence, the maximum allowed by Norwegian law, and has protested that his civil rights are being violated because he doesn't have a good internet connection. Tor said, "Breivik now complains that he can't get the right pencil." Tor doesn't understand the American system, however: "In the United States, it's ridiculous. Why not let them go back into society and be fine?"

I'm shocked at how humanely the Norwegians have treated a mass murderer like Breivik, considering most politicians in the United States would vote to put him to death.

Even so, New York City is looking to Norway now that it's closing the notorious prison at Rikers Island and trying a new model.

Perhaps this compassion is because Norway is on the edge of the world, as Jan said, and one of the least populated countries with only fourteen people for every square mile. The mountains, the sea, the cold, and the darkness can be treacherous enough, so why not stick together and show a bit of humanity?

Flyskam

Flight Shame

EILIF AND I HAD JUST ARRIVED in Norway, and we were already feeling a sense of guilt for the long flight.

"*Flyskam*," our friend Inger explained, "is the new movement of 'flight shame,'" named for all the fuel burned when you fly that destroys the environment. Apparently, one flight can pollute more than a whole year's worth of a person's recycling, composting, and conserving resources. Many in Scandinavia claim to be cutting down on unnecessary travel to avoid sending more carbon into the atmosphere and ruining the planet. Inger assured us that we shouldn't feel guilty about traveling overseas to Norway, but how could we not?

I'd heard vacations are protected by law in Norway, so I had my doubts they could avoid flying. "Leisure time is respected by the government," Kari, a professor in Bergen, had told me. Norwegians take advantage of nature, she said, "and we have the money to enjoy it. We have three weeks of continuous vacation." Employers are required to give employees at least twenty-five days of paid vacation annually.

Jan told me that most people usually get five weeks of vacation on top of regular Christmas and Easter vacation days. Plus they have national holidays for Ascension Day, Pentecost, and other festival days I couldn't place on a calendar. At sixty years of age, most people get an extra week of vacation and yet another at age sixty-five. That's seven weeks of vacation! Even farmers get vacation when "substitute farmers" take care of their crops and animals to give them a break.

Norwegians we met talked about their weeks-long family vacations they took every year, and they asked us where we go on vacation. Of course we were in Norway at the time, but our family has only been able to travel when I tag it onto a work project like this. We'd love to travel every year for pure fun.

"Well, how much vacation do Americans get?"

I explained that there's no such law in the United States but that most employers will grant a couple of weeks off a year. They were shocked when I said that friends from the Midwest only take a long family vacation every few years. I realized that having regular, long vacations enshrined in law by Norway's government must have something to do with happiness. Now, however, Norwegians have to deal with "flight shame" and the environmental guilt.

I learned that Syden, or "the South," is synonymous with these vacations, as many Scandinavians migrate to escape the dreary, dark winters for some sunlight in the Mediterranean. This is where Norwegians come alive due to the five S's intrinsic to Syden: *sjø, sand, sol, sex, og sprit,* or "sea, sand, sun, sex, and spirits." I'd heard that Scandinavians are notorious once they get out of the rigid rules of the north and feel free in the warm south. Petter, the bus driver from Trondheim, explained that on vacations to Syden, "Norwegians make themselves comfortable, or they '*kose seg,*' which can also mean something . . . um . . . well, how do I put it without being vulgar?" Is "happiness" just a euphemism for sex?

I learned that one hundred million people in the north of Europe go south every year, making it the largest annual exodus in the world. Having lived through one gloomy Norwegian winter when Eilif was a baby, I understood the lure of the sunny south to stay sane.

Whole Norwegian communities have been established in Spain and other "low-cost countries," as the Norwegians call them. When I was in Trondheim, I had met a man named Steinar, but he moved to the Canary Islands. He retired at age sixty-two when his wife died, so he moved south with his two children. "There's a whole Norwegian community there, and the kids even go to Norwegian school, which has three hundred students and classes until tenth grade." Steinar joked that his Norwegian friends live down there but come back to Norway to have kids since the Norwegian government has better benefits.

Magne Hatlevik, who now lives in Minnesota, said he "left Norway in 1976 and didn't go back until 1981. Then I noticed it had already started to change." He barely recognized modern Norway and gave the example of his brother-in-law in Norway, who laid lines for the phone company and has now retired at age sixty-four. His wife, Magne's sister, retired at fifty-five. "Still, they take fancy vacations every year," Magne said. "I grew up in a poor country, born in 1951, and we believed that work would make you a better person, but now I see that modern Norway isn't that way. We thought that only the very rich would ever vacation in Mallorca, but now that's standard."

With Scandinavia's high standard of living and low amount of winter sunlight, I imagined it would be hard for them to resist seeking warmer zones. I felt a bit less guilty about our plane trip overseas and also because Eilif and

I would board the coastal steamer Hurtigruten to go to Trondheim rather than board a shameful plane.

Before the departure, Jan and Tonja took us to visit her sister Anna and husband Svein and their fourteen-year-old son Adrian, who had a new video game to show us. Their beautiful little suburban house is like a wooden cabin tucked into a hill. Even though many other houses surround their home, the windy roads and greenery make for a neighborhood of perfectly cozy, or *koselig,* cottages as opposed to so many of America's soul-crushing suburban tract houses with obscene three-car garages and identical beige vinyl siding.

Anne and Svein invited us in and offered us tea, coffee, or Solo orange pop. Adrian brought Eilif over to see their new virtual reality headset that hooks into their videogame console. Eilif put on what looked like a white motorcycle helmet with a blank, white eye guard that made him bump into walls when fictitious butterflies and stingrays floated by him.

Anne told us how Svein had woken her up in the middle of the night when he was moving furniture aside to avoid bumping into the walls and the sofa. He finally just moved the sofa and coffee table away from the screen so he could keep playing. She was very annoyed: "This had better be good."

Svein gave her the virtual reality helmet to put on. "Oh! This is something." Essentially they could now go anywhere on earth. Actual travel was irrelevant. Was this the cure for *flyskam*? Anne wanted to touch, taste, and smell, though. Tonja recommended that she just take off the mask and see what was truly around her.

I put on the helmet and saw how this 3D world was captivating indeed. Nausea swept over me in this virtual world, and I realized my body much preferred actual reality. Eilif forgot his jet lag and became completely absorbed in this new world. He bonked into the wall, tables, and couches and couldn't be drawn back to Norway.

Somehow the conversation veered toward the Norwegian lottery, Norsk Tipping, which gives its profits to support sports and culture. I asked if the winners would be shunned if they couldn't help flaunting their new wealth by buying a castle in Spain. I teased them that they should think like some Americans and get as rich as possible and show off.

Anne joked that Jan had his list of things he'd do with all the money. Svein said, "All I need is right here," and he hugged her.

"BING! The winner!" Anne announced. "I think people should only be able to have a certain amount of wealth."

Tonja leaned to me and said, "Many people in Norway think like this."

"Yes, but wouldn't it be nice to have an apartment in London and Paris as well?" Jan wondered.

Anne replied, "Why? Couldn't you just stay in a hotel when you're there?"

Jan dreamed of a bigger home where they could spread out a bit more.

Anne said, "I don't know why we'd move and wait for three years of construction while someone builds our dream house. Rather than waste all that time, why not buy something already built?"

Svein said, "I'm happy right here."

"BING! Once again the winner," Anne said and gave him a kiss.

Meanwhile, Adrian and Eilif were lost in their virtual reality world. Svein and Anna say that, now with all the heat of global warming, "Spain and Syden are all too hot. We'll just vacation in Nordfjord and go fishing."

I joked that he could get a virtual reality fishing program and wouldn't need to leave home.

"Even then you wouldn't catch anything!" Jan teased.

"I heard of a man near here who sold everything—his apartment, car, everything!—to move out to a *hytte* [cabin] in the mountains," Tonja said. "He said he was finally happy."

"Happy?" Jan asked. "To be happy we need other people."

"BING!" said Tonja.

Black Metal and Stave Churches

"I WISH I WERE ENGLISH," Eilif told me because of his obsession with British music and all the cool styles. I wished exactly the same thing when I was a teenager, but I was sure that Norway had great music and style too. We do have some long-lost British relatives, but I wanted him to appreciate his Norwegian background, which wasn't as showy as the Brits. Eilif and I discussed all sorts of English bands and how groups like the Sex Pistols shocked with outrageous hijinks.

I wanted to show Eilif what it means to be Norwegian, but all the knickknack shops along the wharf in Bergen were full of tacky plastic and wooden Viking souvenirs for kids to remember their trip to the frozen north and take home to terrorize their siblings and pets. One store in an old tar-scented warehouse offered slick steel swords and shields at a thousand dollars a pop. I asked, "When would anyone ever use a razor-sharp, three-foot-long saber?"

Then I remembered when Katy and I were in Bergen with baby Eilif in his stroller. When we had wheeled Eilif into the castle courtyard of Håkonshallen, arrows whizzed near the stroller. Men dressed in bearskins with oversized metal helmets shot arrows from their crossbows at hay bales made to look like enemy knights from Europe, while hollering Vikings covered in chain mail swung giant swords and axes at each other's shields.

"Umm, I don't think this is the best place for a baby," Katy said as we hurried out of the courtyard, away from the reenactment of Viking pillaging.

I remembered the travel guide Magne, who came from near Ålesund, exaggerating, "Everyone traces their family back thirty-seven generations to the first Norwegian king in western Norway." I suppose we could do the same, but our early relatives were poor *husmenn* working on the Drægni farm and living in a shack by an overflowing river.

In Minnesota, we're very familiar with this Viking obsession, since more than three hundred businesses include "Viking" in their names and many claim Norse explorers made it well into the Midwest. Somehow we accept the inconsistency that both Christianity and pagan Viking backgrounds can live in harmony. We ignore violent proselytizers like Olav Tryggvason, whose statue in the center of Trondheim offers either the cross of Christianity or death by his sharp sword.

Eilif was surprised that religion even exists anymore. I told him that Ada, the daughter of our friends he stayed with in Oslo, had invited us to her confirmation. He was confused about her joining the church. "Why would she do that?"

Her mother, Inger, had explained that Ada wanted to have a big party as part of the confirmation process. "Even so . . . why?" Eilif wondered. I think he was secretly relieved that the confirmation would take place after we returned home.

Most kids in Norway we met had no interest in going to church; however, I did remember meeting a teenager in the Sognefjord who was excited about confirmation for one reason: the money.

At the same time, all Norwegians are automatically members of the Lutheran Church of Norway. As we walked through Bergen, Jan explained, "As soon as you are born, the government signs you up." I told him that in the United States we'd be outraged if the government involuntarily registered us to be a certain religion.

"If you don't want this in Norway, you must sign up to become a member of another church and the money will go there. Even if you are an atheist, you can have the money go to that organization, as long as they are organized. Even if you believe in the Flying Spaghetti Monster, the money can go there, as long as it is registered." Each religion gets money from the government based on how many members it has.

I was surprised, since Scandinavia always seemed so secularized—I saw the front page of a Norwegian newspaper announce that a Swedish bishop declared the Bible is merely poetry. He said it has wise tales to teach us but shouldn't be taken as absolute "truth." I was also surprised to hear that Norway has a religion tax, as opposed to the United States, which just allows churches to be tax free.

Our friends Sigrid and Nils from Orkanger near Trondheim didn't want their taxes to go to the Norwegian Lutheran Church. "That's why we're part of a secular organization that gets the money to help out people." Their son was going through confirmation, but not in a church. I tried to understand what he was being confirmed into, but Sigrid only explained, "That happens on Saturdays, not Sundays. They also have secular baptisms too if you want."

Jan explained that the tax is only about eighty dollars per person per year. "Only 1 percent of the population goes to church regularly, but 70 percent are members," he said. "Surely the church would cease to exist in Norway if it weren't for the government, or at least it would be in a vastly different form."

Bergen and western Norway were nicknamed the Bible Belt of Norway because more than 5 percent regularly go to church. Jan said the church is constantly trying to get new members. "If you move to a new town, you will get a note from the local parish for the church there. They know where you are!"

Even so, church attendance is at an all-time low. Magne told me, "We don't really go to churches anymore, just for Christmas and confirmation."

Jarle, the teacher from Oslo, worried about the drop in churchgoers: "What do you believe in in the end? Just in myself? Where do you find comfort, support? What happens when things don't always go well? And there will always be that time."

"The bishops are happy as long as everyone is paid," Tor told me, a bit cynically. He pointed out that even if many people don't attend church, "Norway has more missionaries per capita than any other country." Because of the government's support, "the churches don't need cleaning because so few Norwegians go to church. The churches have never looked so nice."

Norwegian churches have become symbols of the nation's culture. I'd visited several of the twenty-eight surviving stave churches in Norway and learned that many of the Viking legends and heroes had been magically transformed into Christian stories and characters. The dragons became devils, and the pagan Viking hero turned out to be Jesus all along. The guide in the Lom stave church said that the original Catholic ceremonies in the church lasted only five to ten minutes in the mostly dark church with few pews. When the Lutherans took over, suddenly the services stretched two and a half hours, so more windows were cut in the walls to allow light in for parishioners to read the hymns.

I convinced Jan to take Eilif and me to visit the Fantoft stave church in Bergen since this church had originally been built in Fortun around 1150 in the Lusterfjord, where my relatives lived on the Drægni farm. Even though Eilif didn't see the point of religion, perhaps an understanding that our ancestors would regularly file into this stave church a block away from the farm would make an impression.

I'd seen a photo of the church from the late 1800s when it was still in Fortun, and it looked like a windowless three-story wooden barn with a steeple. I'd asked my Norwegian relative from the area, Magne Drægni, who now lives in Bodø, why the town of Fortun let their beautiful church be moved to Bergen. "*Penger!*" he said and gave the universal hand gesture for money. Plus, the little town got a brand new white church while Bergen got a new tourist site.

Eilif, Jan, and I walked through the dense woods that lead to the church in the suburbs of Bergen. The Fantoft stave church looks nothing like the photo from the 1800s, but instead has numerous rooflines, an open porch surrounding the building, and dragons jutting out from the eaves of the church. This is much more "Norwegian," even if it's a fantasy version of what someone imagined Norway to be.

"You know that someone burned it down, right?" Jan told us.

"This is clearly a rebuilt version," I replied.

"Fantoft was set on fire by a Satanist, a black metal musician who called himself 'The Count,'" Jan continued.

"Wait. What?" Suddenly Eilif was interested.

I started reading about *svartmetall,* or "black metal," which more or less began with a group of musicians who met in the early '90s in an Oslo record store, Helvete (Hell), which was decorated with medieval weapons and had a dingy, dungeon-like basement where some would sleep. With warm and fuzzy band names like Mayhem, Hades Almighty, and Thou Shalt Suffer and members sporting black-and-white "corpse" paint to look like zombies or Alice Cooper, these groups sought to shock. They declared themselves "Satanists," whatever that means, and even more evil than those dainty Swedish death metal bands. The Norwegian tabloids ate it up. In the book *Lords of Chaos,* they described themselves as "militant misanthropic Devil worshippers who wanted to spread hatred, sorrow and evil." Musicians took on nicknames like Occultus, Faust, Count Grishnackh, Dead, Hellhammer, and Necrobutcher.

The book *Northern Black Metal Legends* details an interview with one of the ringleaders, Euronymous, who declared the musicians were opposed to "compassion, peace, happiness and fun." Clearly this is not the happiness for which Norway is famous. Perhaps to prove how evil he was, when Euronymous discovered the body of his bandmate from Mayhem dead from a self-inflicted gunshot wound, he took a photo of the scene and put it on the cover of his next record.

Many black metal musicians were obsessed with a return to the brutality of the Vikings and to Norwegian roots before Christianity, which ironically coincides with the idea behind *nasjonalromantikken,* or the "national romantic" movement of the mid-1800s that glorified, and sugarcoated, Norway's past. A century before, Kaiser Wilhelm II regularly vacationed on the Sognefjord and dedicated gargantuan statues of Vikings that the locals felt compelled to erect. Many of these modern musicians would have agreed with the kaiser and took it a step further with a disturbing Nazi bent.

Several of the black metal musicians wanted to return to the Viking age, even if their music was a far cry from anything resembling medieval music. Apparently, Christianity was a poke in the eye to true Norwegianness, so several musicians burned down churches, including the Fantoft stave church. Jan pointed out, "This makes no sense since these stave churches represent the Viking pagan traditions and the parishioners just plopped a cross on top to make it 'Christian.'"

"The Count," Varg Vikernes, likely burned down the church and took a photo of the smoldering cinders for the cover of his next record, *Aske* (Ashes). He later told the newspaper *Dagbladet* that one of the reasons for the arson was to attract more customers to the record store in Oslo. *Really?* I wondered. *Just to sell more records?*

Vikernes was eventually caught for setting fire to other churches across the country and for murdering fellow black metal musician Euronymous. Jan told me that Vikernes had 150 kilos of dynamite when the police arrested him in Bergen and that he was planning on flattening Nidarosdomen, the cathedral in Trondheim.

Vikernes was thrown in a cushy Norwegian jail but then complained to the authors of *Lords of Chaos* that prisons in Norway are too comfortable: "It's much too nice here. It's not hell at all. . . . I asked the police to throw me in a real dungeon, and also encouraged them to use violence." He's already out of jail and living in France, where he was caught stockpiling weapons. I told Eilif we had to leave Bergen and get to Trondheim to see this cathedral before a black metal musician blows it up. I didn't tell Eilif what I read about black metal—I suppose I am censoring what it means to be Norwegian as well, since there's nothing more *norsk* than *svartmetall,* unfortunately.

The Oil Fund and the Welfare State

AFTER TWO DAYS IN BERGEN, Eilif and I boarded the coastal steamer bound for Trondheim, and I put on my swimsuit to relax in the outdoor hot tub and watch the sun try to set over Bergen around midnight. Eilif protested about my plan, "But there's no one out there on the deck."

"Exactly! We'll have it all to ourselves," I replied as the six hundred other people on the boat stayed inside. We had the cheapest room on the entire ship with no windows and only breakfast included. Even if our finances told me otherwise, at least we could pretend we were living the Norwegian high life.

After twenty minutes in our dark room playing the guitar, Eilif finally joined me in the hot tub. He slipped into the bubbly water, and I knew he was getting his bearings when he inexplicably blurted out, "Wait a minute! How is it that no one catches Clark Kent. I mean, he steps into a phone booth and everyone can see his outline. He steps out as Superman. Really? No one has ever figured that out?"

"Very good point," I agreed. "Did you notice the sunset?"

Eilif looked around at the sky turning every shade of

orange to purple and reflecting on the seven mountains of Bergen.

"Whoa . . . yeah!"

I felt decadent, especially since Katy and I couldn't afford much of anything when we had lived here with baby Eilif. We had shopped at the Fretex Salvation Army or the *loppemarked* (flea market) on the weekends. Ironically, Eilif now loves the Fretex.

My great-grandfather Ellef couldn't have imagined this luxury when he fled Norway's abject poverty for the promise of America. Now that Norway has risen from the poorest country in Europe to the richest, I imagined that many Norwegians went on mad spending sprees. Instead I found many are still frugal with their savings. When I had asked Jana and Vidar, a couple I had met in Trondheim, about how often they go out to restaurants, they replied, "Oh, we do go out to eat, but only about once or twice a year." Norway vies for the top spot as the most expensive country in the world. Gasoline is four to five times the price in Minnesota, a pack of cigarettes carries almost six dollars in tax, and sales tax is 25 percent (but on liquor it's much higher).

An American friend living in Oslo put it this way: "It's not that we buy more things or have more things, it's that we are guaranteed a high standard of living. We don't have two cars, we take the bus, and we can probably count the number of times we go out to eat." For the previous few years, Norway could boast the highest quality of life of any nation because of generous social services and the redistribution of wealth. The highest cost of living paired with the highest quality of life hardly makes for an extravagant lifestyle, however.

Norwegians I'd met seem to have an incredible sense of

fairness about their personal wealth, to the point that everyone's personal income is public knowledge and listed on the internet. I assumed that these shy Scandinavians were very respectful of each other's privacy, but several Norwegian friends admitted to checking coworkers' incomes. The government has recently changed this so citizens can't anonymously look up others' income but must sign in so everyone knows who is looking up their income.

Katy and I had lived in Italy for a few years before Eilif was born and noticed that the Italians didn't have the same expectation that everything would be fair like the Norwegians do. Italians weren't surprised (or pleased) by scandal, and everyone knew that Italian businesses routinely kept double books, one was a record to show the tax authorities and the other a secret ledger of the real income listing who is paid under the table. Even ex-Italian prime minister Silvio Berlusconi unwittingly revealed how he became the richest man in Italy: "If reasonable taxes are demanded, no one thinks about avoiding paying them. But if you ask 50 percent or more . . . I consider myself morally justified to do everything I can to avoid paying them."

This is not the same in Norway. Even with high taxes, Norwegians seemed strangely proud to pay them. "I find tax evasion extremely dishonorable, particularly on a corporate scale," Joffe of Trondheim had told me. "I'm very proud to pay tax. The money is in most cases put to very sensible use such as publicly financed education, health care, libraries, support for disabled and unemployed people, and so on."

These taxes pay for the liberal social welfare system that leads to the highest standard of living and best social services in Europe. Income tax weighs in at 38 percent and up to 47 percent. U.S. taxes top out at 37 percent, even for billionaires, who surely have tax shelters to avoid paying most of it.

The disparity between the very rich and the very poor in the United States wasn't always so gaping. According to an article in the *New Yorker,* "By the seventies, America was as equal as any of the Scandinavian countries are today." The studies showed that this equality in the United States unraveled beginning with the Reagan tax cuts.

This all made me wonder whether Katy and I should have tried to stay in Norway after Eilif's birth. The economist Tor Dahl told me: "Norway and the United States are about equal in burden of taxes for federal, state, and local sources. It averages to about 40 percent in both countries." Sales tax is built into the price in Norway. Taxes in the United States used to be up to 94 percent for the billionaires but have plummeted, allowing the wealth gap to explode. Rather than pay Norway's modest top tax of 47 percent, "the richest man in Norway took everything and went to Switzerland," Tor told me. "He's essentially the bogeyman in Norway." This idea that he couldn't share his wealth with others made him a pariah.

In the United States the term "welfare state" may be a dirty word, but the Norwegian equivalent, *velferdsstaten,* often raises nationalist pride in Norway. "It's the system we have chosen," Sissel, a teacher of Norwegian in Trondheim, had told me, "and I'm happy to pay the taxes for it." Some predict that all this money will eventually run out since 52 percent of GDP is put into the public sector.

I'd never met anyone who was happy for taxes, but the benefits were soon clear. Norway's system offers its citizens a degree of stability and certainty unheard of in the United States. A professor of education from Bergen told me, "More people have enough and more than enough. They feel economically safe. We are not walking in constant fear." In the United States, on the other hand, the fear of bankruptcy or of other economic catastrophes is unfortunately common. Death and taxes may be unavoidable, but in Norway at least you get your health care, higher education, and pension provided by the government, and workers won't be out on the street if they lose their job.

Eilif and I sat in the hot tub looking out at the vast expanse of the North Sea, where the riches of Norway were discovered in 1969. At the time Norway was still among the poorest countries in Europe, but then black gold flowed. The sea that swallowed so many sailors and fishermen was now giving back. Is Norway now the land of opportunity?

I had assumed the main reason for Norway's current success was the trillion dollars saved in the government's *oljefond,* or oil fund, but every Norwegian I met vehemently refuted my argument. Inger told me that Norway's current status "comes out of hard work and luck."

Her husband, Knut, pointed out that this fund is thanks to Farouk al-Kasim, an oil engineer from Iraq who married a Norwegian. He knew Norway had to get foreign investment to establish the drilling technology but knew not to sell it to a foreign country and to plan wise investments early on. Inger chimed in, "This was a stroke of luck. We could have handled the wealth in a different way. In Africa or other places, they sell their resources and then it's privatized."

Tor explained to me, "The original drillers came from abroad but were all taxed at 95 percent. All the resources under the Norwegian ocean belonged to the Norwegian people." The idea of a few entrepreneurs becoming super rich and then stashing their cash in Swiss banks didn't fly in Norway. Instead, the ideals of social democracy pushed for the wealth from the huge oil reserves found in the North Sea to be redistributed. A nationalized oil company, Statoil, now called Equinor, was set up with the revenue going into the *oljefond* to support the government rather than the Rockefellers.

"Norway is rich not only because of Statoil," Knut told me, "but also because as a country we've made a decision to share our resources with each other. Like Sweden and Finland, we're founded on a fusion between social solidarity and a democratic ideal. Therefore we don't have the poor like you do in the United States—or the crime, for that matter." I wanted to defend the U.S. system but knew that the problem of allowing the big oil companies to use our natural resources for their own profit didn't trickle down to the rest of us, except in Alaska, where the state government pays each resident a certain amount from the companies.

"We've had a system of public trust," Knut added. "We're not like Saudi Arabia that just kept the money and hired slaves." Foreigners do fill about 10 percent of Norwegian jobs, and about half of all janitorial and maid jobs are done by non-Norwegians, but they are entitled to many of the same benefits as Norwegians.

If the trillion-dollar oil fund was distributed over the five million inhabitants of Norway, this would mean two hundred thousand dollars per person. This money would swamp the economy, so "the government is only allowed to use 3 percent of the oil fund every year to balance the budgets," Sissel, my Norwegian teacher in Trondheim, told me. "I think most people pay their taxes and fees with pleasure knowing that they get so much back: free education through college, a generous pension, free hospital treatment, generous parental leave of one year at full pay."

The irony is that this extremely environmentally conscious country has become fabulously wealthy from polluting fossil fuels. Norway is now the second largest exporter of natural gas and produces 3 percent of the world's oil. What's more, Norway still has ninety billion barrels of oil left to be tapped under the ocean.

To try to make up for the damage from the oil, the Norwegian government has deemed that the oil fund "can't be invested in tobacco, fracking, or ammunition, but only ethical investments," Jarle, the teacher in Oslo, told me. "We've invested heavily in hydro power, high tech, batteries, curing cancer. . . . Norway is the only major country with no foreign debt."

Ninety-nine percent of the electricity in Norway comes from renewable sources, and the oil is exported. Someday this oil will run out or the Norwegians will choose to leave it under the ocean. Even so, compound interest of the oil fund will only get bigger. No wonder the Norwegians didn't seem to be so worried about money.

Å gå viking

To Go "Viking"

IN OUR DARK CABIN aboard the ship, Eilif tried to sleep off his jet lag but was never going to adjust, since we had no windows and therefore no sunlight. I kept trying to rouse him with no luck, so I went upstairs and stared out the windows toward the Sognefjord. I reminisced about when Katy and I brought Eilif as a baby on the regular passenger boat, "Captain of the Fjord 1," fifteen years ago.

This time, I opted against spending a week taking teenage Eilif up the fjord to visit the old shack where his great-great-grandfather Ellef lived, partially because Eilif had been there as a newborn but also because parts of the Sognefjord had become packed destinations for oversized charter buses hauling day-trippers to quaint towns surviving on "Viking tourism." Never mind that "to go Viking" essentially meant to go marauding and returning with stolen loot.

Years ago, I used to love these tacky tourist traps, so I had convinced Katy to bring baby Eilif to the end of one branch of the Sognefjord, the Nærøyfjord, and to the tiny town of Gudvangen. We had reservations at the Gudvangen Fjordtell, which advertised itself as a "Viking Hotel," as if these berserkers had a long tradition of welcoming visitors without butchering them. I suppose the Vikings had to rob the money, but now tourists willingly spend more than eleven billion dollars each year in Norway.

The waterway wove between the ruggedly tall mountains. Waterfalls plunged from the tops of the cliffs down into the salt water of the fjord. Houses were cut into the mountains high up with no visible road or path.

Some of the buildings in Gudvangen Fjordtell attempted to resemble old Viking hovels with grass on the roof of the round, mound-like structures, but the cement and glass gave away the modernist tendency of Norwegian architecture. Grieg's "In the Hall of the Mountain King" was piped into the speakers—followed soon afterward by "Achy Breaky Heart." No matter what the music, I could sit for hours watching the view of four waterfalls from the skylight of our Viking room.

One wall displayed a giant wooden outline of a fjord with an inset mirror that represented water, over which a Viking boat glided. Another wall was covered with wooden axes, swords, and shields, and the bedposts were carved to look like dragons jutting off the bow of a Viking ship. The beds were covered with rough cowhides, but Katy was unimpressed. "What are we supposed to do with this?"

"Apparently, this is to get the true Viking experience," I explained. "Even though I'm pretty sure they didn't have many cows."

"Well, I'm not sleeping with some dead animal on top of me!"

We went for an early dinner at the giant wooden lodge with two-story glass windows overlooking the fjord. Solid banquet tables were surrounded by giant wooden chairs with ornate hand-carved designs from the stave church at Urnes. Whole log banisters lined the stairway to the balcony above, where more cowhides were hung down next to wooden shields and plaster of Paris reliefs of Viking heads to recreate a rustic Viking feel for the recently built inn. The bar offered expensive shots of liquor with fruity flavors and godlike names: Odin, Tor, Loke, and Idun (the goddess who guarded the gods' apples).

Katy, baby Eilif, and I were the only people in the enormous restaurant, so our talkative waiter, Alessandro, from Turin, Italy, took the time to tell us all about Gudvangen. "In a couple of years, they hope to make this a UNESCO World Heritage site. Last year, they had a Viking market— you know, of all the craftsmen making swords and all that— for the first time in seven hundred years."

"How's the food here? Is it Viking food?" I asked.

"It is Norwegian food," he replied a bit dismayed. Then he whispered, "Actually the food is more German because of the 'executive chef' and his brother, 'the assistant.' I am just one of the cooks." As he pronounced each of the titles, his lips pursed together and his whole face tensed like he was chewing fish heads.

"How is it being Italian working for a German head chef?" Katy asked.

"It's a very bad situation in the kitchen," he replied bitterly.

"So we shouldn't eat here?" I asked, knowing full well that it was the only restaurant in town.

"Don't worry, I will take care of you," he said, as if he were protecting us from being poisoned by the German cook.

"We trust you," Katy said, and Alessandro didn't seem to take the responsibility lightly.

As he went back into the kitchen, I told Katy maybe

we'd get true Viking fare. I said, "They often ate their meat raw and drank fresh warm blood."

She looked at me disgusted. "Why are you telling me this?"

"I was just wondering what would happen if they served true Viking food."

Alessandro returned with two plates of pork topped with a creamy sauce and red cabbage and mixed vegetables on the side. "It's Norwegian food, but I made this myself, so it's OK," he assured us and stole a menacing glance at the German in the kitchen.

He waited as we tasted it and nodded our approval. It was excellent and perhaps the best "Norwegian" meal we'd had during our entire year. I told him so, but he shook his head and held up his index finger to stop me.

"No. Now you flatter me," Alessandro replied. He then rubbed his chin and thought for a minute. "Yes, that could be possible."

As he skipped back into the kitchen perhaps ready to take on the chef, I told Katy maybe we'd found Viking heaven after all. "You know when Vikings died and went to Valhalla, they feasted on the boar Særimne, who they could eat, and he'd reappear the next day ready to be eaten again."

"Will you stop it?" she said. "Why are you doing this? I just want to enjoy my meal without thinking about the damn Vikings."

At the end of the meal, Katy went back to our room with Eilif and I ran into Alessandro having a cigarette outside the entrance to the lodge next to a skinny mannequin of a Viking with long eyelashes and a pink face with a bloody slash down the right cheek. A horned helmet was plopped over the statue's blond wig, and long leather boots fit snugly up to the calves, but any sign of the legs was obscured by the belt that was pulled down below the hips.

"Who's this?" I asked

"This Viking's name is George," he said. "Actually, it's a female model. You can tell from the breasts." Alessandro looked at George admiringly. "We just covered him with a beard. Maybe he should be called 'Georgette.'" Poor Georgette's sword was stuck in a birch log like the sword in the stone, relegating the androgynous Viking to chopping wood rather than slaughtering foreigners.

A bit closer to the parking lot, a rough wooden sculpture of a Viking guarded a couple of Volvos. A plaque at the bottom was inscribed with the text "Utformet med STIHL" (made with Stihl chainsaws). Alessandro said, "This Viking doesn't have a name. He came from up at the intersection there. Now the chainsaw artist is going to do a whole series of Viking statues because over there, they'll build a Viking lodge like the one in Lofoten."

In the distance, the roar of a diesel-spouting tour bus came echoing down the valley toward the Viking Hotel. Alessandro stubbed out his cigarette and said, "I must go now. You see, after June 1 the season begins, and often five buses will come all at once. Sometimes we must serve a meal to one thousand people in one hour. It's completely crazy."

Alessandro hurried inside to start cooking, and I watched the tourist bus arrive. A woman in a pin-striped business casual suit stepped off the bus first, obviously the group leader, and announced, "We only have ten minutes before the boat leaves!" Within minutes, a group of Brits had me taking photos of them in front of the chainsaw sculpture. Other tourists scurried into the gift shop and came out minutes later brandishing plastic swords and wearing plastic

Viking helmets with blond braids as if they were ready to act out a Wagner opera.

Now fifteen years later, this entire area of Nærøyfjord has been designated a UNESCO World Heritage site, which only increases the number of tourists descending into the make-believe land of Gudvangen and Flåm. More than nine million tourists visit Norway each year and produce more than 4 percent of the country's GDP.

I thought about my great-grandfather and his desperately poor family who did everything they could to get out of here. Now their history is glorified and commodified. That skeptical view didn't stop me years ago from getting a little helmet and battle-ax for baby Eilif to exalt his ancestry. If I hadn't, we probably wouldn't be in Norway now.

Tunnelfeber

Tunnel Fever

WE ARRIVED AT THE PIER in Trondheim early in the morning, after our two-night trip winding around islands and waterfalls on the coast of the North Sea. Eilif was still jet-lagged, so I let him sleep in while I had breakfast. At ten o'clock, the crew announced our names over the ship's intercom, declaring that we were late to disembark. Maybe we were too lazy to leave this luxurious boat and set off on our adventure.

Our friend Runa met us at the end of the gangplank. She and her husband, Joffe, had agreed to host us for a few days while we rediscovered the city where we had lived for a year. We piled into their fancy, yet cozy VW hybrid, and I hoped to point out the city sites to Eilif on our way to their house. I searched for the apartment we had lived in next to the giant cemetery. Instead, we drove over a new bridge and down into a new tunnel that didn't exist fifteen years ago. Runa explained that Trondheim has several new tunnels to help alleviate traffic and make the city more pedestrian friendly, and this one is nearly three kilometers long under the city. City planners built a similar tunnel on the other side of town too.

Runa told us about a new syndrome in Norway, *tunnelfeber,* or "tunnel fever," the claustrophobia of being un-

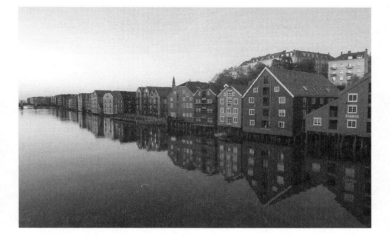

derground in these lengthy car caves but also the mania of spending the country's money on more and more tunnels. I imagined that Norwegians were becoming like the trolls in Grieg's "In the Hall of the Mountain King" in the Dovrefjell mountains, hoarding their gold, or their trillions from the oil fund, in these endless tunnels.

I remembered when the tour guide Magne asked, "Who wants to see Norway from the inside?" and added, "That's called Norwegian oil money at work—another tunnel!"

I'd traveled through many of the superlong tunnels around the Sognefjord that connect these beautiful areas to the rest of the world. It probably took my great-grandfather Ellef close to a week to go the 127 miles up the Sognefjord to his family's *hytte*; now it could be done in an afternoon. I remembered when Katy and I had talked to a woman at the tourist desk in Bergen who recommended we take the route up the Sognefjord through tunnel after tunnel. The woman exclaimed excitedly that if we take the bus, "you'll even go through the longest tunnel in the world from Lærdal to

Aurland. It has artificial blue lights to make it look like day-time, and the road even spirals inside the mountain!"

I had tried to interrupt her, but she held up her index finger for me to wait while she told me more. She read from a brochure, "'It's 24.5 kilometers long and 7.5 kilometers longer than Switzerland's longest tunnel at St. Gotthard.' Just don't think about the quarter mile of rock above your head!" She kept her finger up to keep me from speaking as she researched more: "I'm sorry, but none of the tunnels in the Sognefjord go under glaciers."

Because of the bounty from the oil fund, Norway has been able to make fantastic tunnels and bridges to connect remote areas so people don't need to move to the cities for modern services or to take lengthy ferries. Magne had told me that he came from an island near Ålesund, but now the ferries are fewer since more bridges connect nearby islands. He said that people on his island now ask, "Where will I meet my neighbors?" They used to spend hours on the fer-ries chatting, but now everyone is protected by their cars.

Magne told me that Norway's tunnel fever has reached a point where they're working on "*et hull i havet,*" a hole in the ocean. Just south of Ålesund is the westernmost point of Norway, called Stad, where the North Sea is especially treacherous. Over the past hundred years, a ship has sunk nearly every year going around it, so the government is dis-cussing a "ship tunnel" on this stretch to avoid the terri-ble open sea that has led to many deaths and brave rescues. This tunnel will have a canal of water through it to allow the coastal steamers and other large ships to pass through unscathed.

Besides the ship tunnel, Magne pointed out the land bridges over highways built to allow animals free passage without being hit by cars. The government has even made toad tunnels to allow the creatures to cross busy roads without being squashed.

I was amazed at the cost of all these tunnels and bridges, but Petter, the bus driver from Trondheim, told me: "You can't think of it as just the cost of the tunnel, but also how much money you save with time and how many lives are saved by having good roads. For example, north of Trondheim, there is one road to northern Norway. If there is an accident, all of northern Norway is cut off, and we have to take a six-hour detour into Sweden to get there. We are making a second road and the world's longest tunnel."

This immense investment in infrastructure for a nation of just five million is astounding. I imagined what U.S. cities would look like if we tunneled underground rather than bulldozing neighborhoods for bigger highways. Would we have more parks and fewer accidents? A Norwegian friend told me, "First, the United States has to get the money from the oil companies!"

Cooperatives and Conformity

THE SUN NEVER SET but circled over our heads every day in Trondheim. At the end of May, this gentle sunlight gave me constant energy, which I needed to keep up with fifteen-year-old Eilif, who had finally recovered from his jet lag.

Our hosts, Runa and Joffe, had both played in a punk band when younger, and Eilif felt right at home. All Eilif wanted was rock 'n' roll, so he banged away on their piano and took requests as he played David Bowie songs by ear. Joffe let him turn his electric guitar up to 11 and showed him a semi-obscene comic that he'd just had published in a slick alternative magazine. This was teenage heaven.

Joffe showed us a fresh copy of the *Klassekampen* ("class struggle") newspaper, a publication that he told us even journalists at NRK, the national government-funded broadcasting network, respected.

"That seems strange since I don't see any social class struggle here in Norway," I said. "You don't have the homeless or the obscenely rich."

"Of course there's still class," Joffe insisted. "Perhaps it's not as pronounced as in England, but are there those who are richer? More educated? Those with fewer opportunities? Then there's class."

I told him how Eilif and I had just stayed in Bergen with someone from the Høyre party who was amazing at looking up studies and statistics to back up his arguments for this right-of-center party. Joffe wasn't having any of it and quoted a phrase made popular by Mark Twain: "There are three kinds of lies: lies, damned lies, and statistics."

Clearly, Joffe questioned the status quo and refused to blindly obey anyone. This was a refreshing change from the usual answers I had gotten from Norwegians about why they are so "happy." The typical response had tended toward "social cohesion" or "social unity," which seemed disturbingly close to plain old conformity. For example, a couple of weeks earlier, I had asked Petter from Trondheim about all the rules that he has to follow as a bus driver that he didn't like or agree with.

"Yes, all the regulations drive us crazy, but we have to obey the law," he told me. "I've heard that in the United States you say, 'If I don't get caught, I'm not breaking the law.' Is that true? I suppose you just need to look at your president."

"I guess that Norwegians always just want to follow the rules, even if they don't agree with them," the tour guide Magne chimed in. "Just look at Norway's relation with the European Union. Norway isn't even part of the EU but follows the rules of the EU more than any of the actual member countries!" The two of them agreed that Norwegians generally have a certain trust in the system to be fair and beneficial to everyone.

Magne explained that, to understand Norwegians, "you need to know the term 'Slik har de det der,' which is literally

'That's how they got it there,' but means 'That's different.' This is an acceptance of the situation. For example, if you see someone drinking methanol, but you know that's terrible, you say, '*O slik har de det der.*'"

This radical tolerance seems strange and even irresponsible, but Joffe explained to us that the Norway he grew up in wasn't always so lenient. "Skateboards were banned in Norway until 1989!" Stores are still closed on Sundays, for the most part.

Some of the items we consider standard in the United States were strange to them. Eilif asked Runa for a tissue for his runny nose. Runa was surprised that he wanted "nose paper" since she didn't think it sanitary. "We don't blow our noses like the Germans do, who walk around with a moist handkerchief in their pockets."

With these contradictions in mind, Eilif and I prepared to discover this different changed world of Trondheim. Joffe and Runa lent us two bicycles. "It's the best way to see Trondheim," Joffe assured us.

The temperature was shifting dramatically every fifteen minutes, and the weather report showed a cloud icon with a snow/rain mix and sunshine at the same time. "We have all seasons in a day," Runa told us. "If you don't like the weather, wait ten minutes!" Indeed, out the front window we saw rain, the side window had sun, and the back had dark clouds with a double rainbow.

Fifteen years ago, I had only seen the city by pushing baby Eilif in a stroller, or *trilling*, as the Norwegians call it; now we could zip around on bikes. Eilif and I constantly got lost on our ride, but it didn't matter—the fjord is on one side, the river on the other, and the fortress is atop the hill.

Trondheim is a city of pedestrians, but fearless students

on bicycles weren't afraid to whiz by within an inch of us. Most cyclists didn't have bells and were often chatting on cell phones while zooming down the hills. When we heard them coming, we learned never to move too quickly to one side or the other or we'd be a bump in the road for them.

We soon learned the relaxed rhythm of Trondheim, where many of the coffee shops don't even open until 11:00 a.m. This is a university town, where creative students wear outrageous outfits—I'd never seen so many pirate costumes—and even had goofy hazing rituals at the beginning of the school year.

Trying not to imagine Eilif involved in these bizarre initiation rites, I introduced him to the array of pastries at the historic Rosenborg Bakeri from 1902 in the Møllenberg neighborhood. I told Eilif that this was his chance to use his Norwegian that he'd studied for five years at summer camp. He approached the counter, avoided Norwegian, and said in teenaged English, "Um yeah, like, I think I'll maybe have, like, a cinnamon roll, you know?"

I rolled my eyes, but the young Norwegian at the counter understood everything. She seemed interested in this cute young American and responded in perfect English. Perhaps Eilif would fit in after all.

We biked through vast neighborhoods of classic "workers' housing," colorful two- or three-story wooden buildings with cobblestone streets. These wooden flats date to the 1920s, and the government has protected the buildings. Joffe had told us about *boligsamvirke,* or "housing cooperatives," which help keep the rent down and conserve these historic structures.

Norwegian houses have strange characteristics that constantly confuse me: the thresholds on the floor under doors are so tall that I constantly tripped; light switches are typically *outside* of a room; blinds and curtains are rarely sufficient to keep out the constant light in the summer; and everyone takes off their shoes before entering the house, perhaps to feel the toasty warmth from the in-floor heating.

Runa's sister lived in one of these co-op houses with her Swedish husband, who asked me, "Don't you preserve old buildings from the '20s in America, or can they just tear them down and destroy the architecture?" Residents can't renovate anything without permission from the cooperative board, which even controls the colors of the paint they can use.

Eilif was more intrigued by Svartlamoen, an anarchist community of squatters in occupied houses that hosts music festivals and is full of sculptors, artists, and punks. Besides coffee and art, the only other thing I saw for sale in Svartlamoen was the daily left-wing *Klassekampen* newspaper. The colorful murals and political posters showed that all is not lefse and lutefisk in Norway.

We biked back under a rainbow over the little bridge by the *brygge*, or wooden wharf, from the Bakklandet neighborhood into the center of town. We parked our bikes in the shade of the impressive Nidarosdomen, the gothic cathedral where Norwegian kings are crowned and St. Olav's body is (likely) buried. Eilif recognized the outline of the church from the cod liver oil spoon given by our friend Wes to keep him healthy.

My teenager finally perked up when I mentioned that one of the statues on the church was sculpted in the likeness of Bob Dylan. While searching for St. Bob (hint: it's St. Michael on the very top), he was enthralled by the statue of

Bishop Sigurd holding a bowlful of his nephews' disembodied heads.

Inside the west entrance, an organist tested a giant new pipe organ that complements the historic organ in the north wing. The organist occasionally interrupted the ghostly hush of the church with eerie bursts from the bass organ pipes that made my clothes tremble from the vibration. Then, as if descending from heaven, or at least the vaulted ceilings, I heard a familiar melody emanating out of the second organ.

Wait, this wasn't a religious hymn but a rock 'n' roll anthem from the Minnesota band Hippocampus! I looked over to see Eilif pounding away on the keyboard next to the altar, just like the phantom of the opera. I quickly stopped his rock song in this place of worship.

"What does it matter?" he complained.

"You can't just start playing in this church," I said and tried to explain the importance of this cathedral where kings are crowned.

"The cover to the organ was open," he protested. "Besides, they let that other guy play!" After all, isn't this Dylan's church? I wondered why I was trying to make him conform—perhaps he was right to shake things up a bit.

Back on our bikes, we were soon blocked by a hill that was nearly impossible to scale. Fortunately, we discovered the world's only bicycle lift. We watched as the cycling pros put out their foot and a little metal pedal appeared in a track that pushed them up the steep incline. After we tried and failed three times, a cyclist advised us, "Keep a stiff leg"— perhaps the Norwegian equivalent of "Keep a stiff upper lip." When we finally managed, we couldn't compete and only made it halfway each time. Even the skateboarders passed us by. Clearly we needed to cut down on the pastries to survive a vigorous day of biking in Trondheim.

We were on our way to visit a high school where one of my university classmates, Astrid, taught, so Eilif could see a typical school. He was hungry, and the cafeteria was just closing. The salmon burgers were gone, and he wasn't too excited about the other choices of *sodd* (meatball soup) or *grøt* (porridge with cinnamon). Eilif soon told me that he would not fit into this school since all the kids seemed obsessed with clothes and gossip. Astrid agreed that he was essentially right. She then invited us to supper that evening to meet some friends who had a completely different lifestyle.

Since lunch was a bust, and all this rage against the system makes a teenager hungry, we fueled up on Gullbrød, a brand of dark chocolate–covered marzipan, and ingefærøl, spicy ginger ale, both from Trondheim. To recover from the biking and prepare for a big dinner, we relaxed at the Pirbadet pool, where Eilif had done his first *babysvømming,* or "baby swimming," when he was just a few months old—the standard age for swimming lessons for newborn Norwegians. This is simply the best swimming pool ever, complete with saunas, slides, and warm pools looking across the fjord to Munkholmen Island, where monks supplanted the Vikings who used to place severed heads on poles to ward off intruders. "Cool!" Eilif said after I explained the gruesome details.

The kids at the pool effortlessly ignored the posted rules, and the lifeguards didn't bother enforcing them. Strangely, this made the kids take responsibility for their actions. Rather than roping off the highest high dive, a breathtaking ten meters above the water, lifeguards let the

kids scramble up and then decide if they wanted to risk a painful belly flop.

Eilif was content with the warm waterfall, but when he was a baby at this pool, he was intrigued by the raucous boys who used to climb up a large blow-up octopus, twenty feet long from limb to limb, that floated in the main pool. Rather than just scrambling up it and diving off, the kids played king of the hill, or rather king of the octopus.

Some of these boys would stop in the sauna, where the thermostat was set to a sweltering 215 degrees Fahrenheit. I remembered that water boils at 212 degrees and wondered if my blood would boil. Among the cluster of boys, a few showed how tough they were by sitting on the highest, hottest wooden platform. Others couldn't decide if they wanted to be in the sauna or out. As the door opened and shut for each boy's indecision, the temperature thankfully dropped to 180 degrees.

I remembered shielding baby Eilif from these wild boys when a gang of them raced over to the enormous tube slide that spiraled down from the ceiling. Not content with just sitting and sliding, they formed a huge chain with all of them lying face-first on red kickboards. They circled around inside the tubes and splashed into the pool in a big hog pile. Right next to the pool, a big sign prohibited more than one person at a time and absolutely no flotation devices on the slide. That's OK—by the time the lifeguards noticed, the boys were already bored with the slide.

Today with a teenaged Eilif, only a few kids arrived, and they were mostly interested in the little café on the open veranda above the pool. Considering the pool was a sort of fitness club, I thought they would serve health food like granola and energy drinks. Instead the menu consisted of french fries, burgers, and soft-serve ice cream. Eilif was hungry again, but I assured him we'd have a great dinner at our friend's house.

We struggled up the hill again on our bikes and found Astrid's quaint wooden house with a stunning view over Trondheimsfjord. We sat at the table that looked out on the cemetery next to the apartment we lived in when Eilif was a baby. Astrid had a two-year-old girl when we stayed in

Trondheim fifteen years ago and now has another adorable two-year-old girl with her husband. Luckily, he's a musician and has instruments that Eilif played to pass the evening.

Several other friends showed up, and Eilif and I tried to follow the Norwegian conversation as best we could. I complained/bragged about all the biking we did that day, but two of Astrid's friends, Vidar and Jana, had just walked ten kilometers along the coast to get there. They lived and worked at Camphill, one of six planned communities throughout Norway. "The idea began in England, but we have it here in Norway too," Vidar said. Rather than serve in the military when he turned eighteen, years ago he spent a year of civil service working at Camphill.

Now they were taking the year "off" without pay, with their two kids, ages five and twelve, to help people with disabilities farm. "Yes, the Norwegian government allows us families with kids under twelve a year off from work," Jana told me. They have plum jobs at NRK, the Norwegian national broadcasting network, and, yes, they did read the *Klassekampen* newspaper. I also learned that the Norwegian government had banned all other television stations in the country from 1960 to 1981, presumably to control the media's message to the people.

I mentioned that Americans often criticize Scandinavian countries for implementing too many government controls and meddling in people's lives. Jana disagreed and pointed out that she had stayed in Southern California as a student and just went back to visit after twenty-five years. "The difference was stark between the United States and Norway," she said. "I saw my educated friends [in California] had moved home to take care of their parents since they couldn't afford the health care." She said that the family structure is no longer quite so important in Norway because the government will help out.

Astrid told how she's glad that the Norwegian government helps older people with their pensions and health care. "I'm an only child, so I don't want to be the sole caregiver of my parents," she said. "I joke with my parents that if I visit them, they know that it's Christmas."

Jana said that one of the reasons she's back for a year in Trondheim is to be close to her aging father since the government allows for this year off. That and she wanted to get away from the rat race of Oslo. Even though she had spent the day working with chickens, she was impeccably dressed. "They peck me when I try to take their eggs!"

Her husband, Vidar, had harvested apples and then sold the *saft*, or fruit juice, around Trondheim. "It's very popular all around town."

The year on the farm sounded idyllic, but they cautioned me that people are the same everywhere. Vidar said that everyone is supposed to be equal at Camphill, but of course some end up taking the lead to organize.

"All this talk about volunteering is all well and fine," Jana confessed a bit exasperated, "but people just need to be nice!" They were frustrated that this place with such high ideals still has small-minded people. "People can be petty and gossipy, but isn't that everywhere?"

Clearly they liked the community aspect of living on a cooperative farm that provided for everyone. Yes, they had to live communally and hold back their criticism to get along. Soon they had to return to Oslo, the big city. Their twelve-year-old daughter was now worried about going back to the hustle-bustle of consumerism where she was supposed to have all the right things. How would she fit in?

Påskekyllingen

The Easter Chicken

"SO IS IT TRUE? Is Norway really like the myths we have of it in Italy?" my Italian friend Stefano asked me after Katy and I had spent our year in Trondheim. "Are there beautiful tall blond women everywhere? For us in Italy, Norway and Sweden are a paradise we dream of." I usually try not to perpetuate stereotypes but instead told him, "Of course!" Why would I want to destroy his dreams? Some joke that as many as 90 percent of Scandinavian women are blond while not even half of the men are.

Likewise, Norwegians I met often viewed Italy and the Mediterranean as paradise, even if it's a bit too chaotic. "The Italians just like noise. Have you ever noticed that?" Knut told me. "They just honk their horns because they like noise." Still, Norwegians can't get enough of vacationing in Italy.

When I wrote my book about Katy giving birth to baby Eilif outside Trondheim, some of the staff at the Fulbright office in Oslo were not pleased with my description of Norway. "You make us look quaint," Tove at Fulbright complained. She insisted that Scandinavia is modern and sophisticated.

I was confused since I wasn't denying that Norway is modern. "Well, to me, Norway *is* quaint," I said. "This is a compliment."

She wasn't convinced.

I mentioned the grass-roofed cottages, the stave churches, and the national holiday, *syttende mai,* when almost everyone dresses in their national costume. She just shook her head.

To play with this stereotype, Katy and I staged a ridiculous photo for the cover of our book *In Cod We Trust.* I posed in a Norwegian *lusekofte* sweater wearing a rucksack on my back with a thermos of coffee, and Katy was in the traditional dress of a *bunad* sitting on a *spark* (kick-sled) in front of a grass-roofed cottage. Most Norwegians—except for Tove probably—recognized immediately that we were spoofing this cliché. I thought that we should carry a fish too but was outvoted.

Back home, relatives loved the photo: "Oh, so that's the kind of clothes they wear in Norway?"

Another friend said, "I see that Katy and Eric are fitting right in!"

Clearly the silly picture wasn't over-the-top enough, and we perpetuated the stereotypes. When our Norwegian friend Knut saw it, he said, "Well, when you think about everyone going to the mountains for Easter, most people will wear similar costumes, except for the *bunad,* of course."

I assumed that Easter in Norway was filled with flowers and gentle springtime sun. Instead, bookstores sell out of the latest dark *kriminallitteratur,* the famous Nordic crime novels, and people watch grisly television shows. I'm baffled by this obsession with gruesome murders in a country that is notoriously crime free; we can always dream, I suppose. Too much peace and light makes one bored and blind.

Leading up to Easter, stores closed on Thursday and Friday and opened just for a bit on Saturday before closing for two more days. Katy and I hadn't expected this when we lived in Trondheim but fortunately had shopped a bit on Wednesday; otherwise we'd have been out of food. Easter was synonymous with eating. Palm Sunday, previously nicknamed "pork Sunday," was followed by "pork Monday" and "Fat Tuesday," once called "Porridge Tuesday" because everyone filled up on super-creamy *rømmegrøt* to forget the lean times of Lent. An essential delicacy is *påskemarsipan*, the Easter marzipan that requires extra shifts at the Nidar candy factory in Trondheim to meet demand.

Traditionally, Norwegians feasted on the lamb of God for dinner and ate boiled eggs for breakfast. The demand for eggs is so high that they say the hens must work overtime. I explained to Knut about Easter traditions in the United States, but he was surprised. "We don't have an Easter bunny in Norway," he said. "That never really made sense to us. Why would a rabbit bring around eggs? Instead, we have an Easter chicken."

Another holiday that wasn't as serene as I expected was New Year's Eve, which resembled a reenactment of a World War II Axis bombing raid. A giant storefront in downtown Trondheim was transformed into an explosives bazaar with giant fireworks for sale that would easily be illegal back in Minnesota, such as a two-story-tall blow-up doll of a firecracker man.

The holiday isn't just one or two days. It begins with New Year's Eve, *nyttårsaften*, but continues into First New Year's Day, *første nyttårsdag* (January 1), and Second New Year's Day, *andre nyttårsdag* (January 2). As soon as it got completely dark on December 31, which is about three o'clock in the afternoon, the bombs began along with the drinking. These weren't just Roman candles but huge professional fireworks lit by tipsy students. What could possibly go wrong? That year in Trondheim, we hunkered down at home with our baby as constant flashes like a strobe light illuminated our apartment followed by booms that rattled our cupboards.

All these oversized fireworks seemed especially risky around the quaint—yes, quaint—wooden buildings in the Bakklandet neighborhood, but luckily no fire trucks had to weave their way through the cobblestone streets to extinguish any blazes from errant mortar fire. The morning after, the parks and a vacant lot near our apartment looked like a war zone with littered remnants of half-exploded bombs. Soon the snow safely covered up the debris, and by spring the gunpowder would dissolve.

Besides Christmas and New Year's, the most representative festival of Norway is *syttende mai*, literally the seventeenth of May. The occasion marks the signing of the constitution in 1814, when Norway was briefly independent from Denmark and Sweden hadn't taken over. Not until 1905 would Norway again be independent. Jan told me about meeting a Swedish foreign minister who asked him earnestly, "So does Norway still want to be independent?" After all, doesn't everyone want to be Swedish?

Unfortunately, the second paragraph of the original constitution stated that Jews were banned from coming to Norway. This clause wasn't deleted until 1851. Today different ethnic groups wave their own flags as Norway has pushed to become more diverse.

On *syttende mai,* everyone tries to look their best, and that means wearing a *bunad,* or regional folk dress, which can easily cost up to twelve thousand dollars. Runa proudly wore a *bunad* that she found secondhand and fit her perfectly.

"*Du er så heldig!*" (You are so lucky!), her sister told her.

Joffe corrected her, "*Nei, du er så flink*" (No, you are so clever).

Runa thought about it and said, "I'd rather be lucky than clever!"

"At confirmation, people usually get their *bunad* passed down from their grandparents," my classmate Vigdis told me. Another classmate, Astrid, has a *bunad* too but wanted to dispel this myth of the old Norway that refuses to die.

On *syttende mai,* though, all the beauty and stereotypes of Norway are on full display. *Bunad*s are everywhere and strikingly lovely. Sigrid, the midwife who helped deliver baby Eilif, told us she once got called into the hospital on *syttende mai* wearing her *bunad.* "I had to be covered in plastic to keep the *bunad* clean," she recalled about the birth. "The doctor was distracted the whole time and kept looking at me and said, 'You are so beautiful!' He stared at me when he should have been looking at the birth!"

I'd read about an old ritual in Norway where young women put eggs, I assume hard-boiled, in their dresses, and they'd tempt young men to find them. When I asked Norwegian friends about this provocative game, they replied. "They wore many layers of clothes then, so it was OK. It wasn't like today now that they dress like Britney Spears."

These *bunad*s are such a point of pride that friends joked that the "*Bunad* Police" are out to ensure that each one is "correct." These busybodies know exactly what each *bunad* is supposed to look like and who is "allowed" to wear them. The town of Røros even has a special *gammelungkar* ("old bachelor") *bunad*. Runa told me, "You must have a connection to the region of your *bunad*, so many people exaggerate that 'I have a cousin or an aunt from that area,' but it's mostly because they like the design."

Tor told me about a local squadron of the "*Bunad* Police," like Interpol fashionistas, who scrutinized the Norwegian community in the United States because they failed to adhere to the rules. "In Florida, they needed a light *bunad* but were criticized. Who would wear thick wool in that heat?" he said. Still, though, "*bunad*s probably bring people together more than anything else. Immigrants wear them now." Just as I saw other nations' flags waved during *syttende mai*, immigrants sported colorful dresses from Africa and the Middle East.

I liked this debate about what is considered "acceptable" since it gives young people something to rebel against. For the first time, I saw cars parked haphazardly, facing the wrong direction, unusual in Norway, and asked Joffe about this clear violation in such an orderly country. "On *syttende mai*, the laws loosen up for the day," he said but then warned that on this national holiday, "it's a law that you must take down your flag when you go to bed."

The other enforced fun is the *barnetog*, or "children's parade," which is the centerpiece of the whole festival, since Norwegians marched their youngsters out in starter *bunad*s to wave the Norwegian flag when the country was still "occupied" by Sweden, knowing full well that the Swedes would never crack down on a bunch of well-dressed toddlers. "Being in the *barnetog* is mandatory in elementary school," little Oskar told me.

"What if you don't want to?" I asked.

"Well, I don't think that's an option," Oskar replied, as if that was a dangerous question. "Everyone just does it because it's so much fun. When you're in high school you can choose if you want to or not."

Perhaps because Norway's independence can be traced to the courage of these kids in fancy duds, "today, children get to eat as much *is* as they want," Joffe told me. "If a child asks you for *iskrem* [ice cream], you give it to them!"

After lots of flag waving, yelling of "*Hipp, hipp, hurrah!*" and exclaiming "*Gratuler med dagen!*" (Congratulations on the day!), everyone is hungry. Kids eat ice cream, hot dogs (*pølser*), and soda pop, which all seems strangely American to me. I had first learned about these sausages when I mistakenly asked, in my bad Norwegian, for five *poser,* or shopping sacks, at the grocery store, but the clerk offered me five *pølser* instead. Fortunately, *pølse* vendors prepare well in advance for the post-parade rush of hungry festivalgoers. Big dangling containers of mustard and ketchup hang down from a hook, and we milked them like an udder to squirt on the *pølser*.

Despite my journalistic cynicism, I'd never seen such an outpouring of joy, fun, and kindness as on *syttende mai*. I expected garbage everywhere, but when more than one hundred thousand people on the streets went home, I saw a total of two beer cans littered on the ground. The only person who didn't seem happy in all of Norway was the glum king, who appeared on NRK television from his balcony in Oslo and wouldn't even crack a smile or sing the national anthem. "Oh, he's supposed to do that," our friend Kari from Tønsberg told me, since it's a solemn occasion and not to be taken lightly. "If he smiles, it's undignified."

Redhats

EILIF IS CONSIDERING ATTENDING a Norwegian *folke-høgskole,* or "folk high school," in a couple of years or perhaps a Norwegian university with free tuition. We visited the university in Trondheim and got a tour from Sissel, my Norwegian teacher from when we lived here. The campus was quiet as students diligently prepared for their six-hour final exams in each subject. Eilif wasn't too excited about that and was far more interested in the wild graduating high schoolers we bumped into around town as they stumbled around and sang a bit too loudly.

These are the *russ.* They are very loud, are usually drunk, and put on bizarre outfits of red, blue, or black overalls (depending on their academic major) and haze each other in hijinks that would surely be outlawed in the United States.

Russ is short for *russefeiring,* or "graduation celebration," but stems from the Latin *cornua depositurus,* meaning the removal of a horn that first-year university students had to wear on their head until they passed their first-year exams. The practice of *russ* began before the University of Oslo was established in 1812. Prior to then, Norwegian university students had to travel to Copenhagen to go to school. The Norwegian students embraced the odd Danish tradition and adopted it in high schools across Norway and added wearing red or blue clothes right before graduating from high school.

While this may sound honorable, these students are on a mission to have the craziest party with the most outrageous pranks. These teenagers are about to graduate from high school and are given free rein to do anything they wish before entering adulthood. This coming-of-age blowout is a last hurrah of youthful indiscretion before the drudgery of adulthood. Unless someone is hurt, the police just look away. Some of the tricks are baffling (cleaning a kilometer of train track with a toothbrush), while others are brilliant (making giant troll footprints up an entire water tower as if one of these monsters walked clear up to the top). While I would have preferred to have Eilif admire the Norwegians in their *bunad*s, the traditional Norwegian outfits, the job of the *russ* on *syttende mai* is to mock the entire formality of Constitution Day and demand attention. While the *barnetog*, or "children's parade," is the focus of the day, the *russetog*, or "*russ* parade," demands attention. These sleep-deprived, drunk, and/or hungover students march or ride on floats as they sing along with *russ* bands that strive to be the loudest and funniest of them all.

Magne the travel guide complained, "These kids now do too much *russ*. The music is too loud, and they are too crazy."

"And you were never that way, I'm sure!" Petter from Trondheim replied.

I asked Petter about his time as *russ*.

"I don't remember much; I just know that my mom wasn't very proud of me when I was *russ*. She said that at the *russetog* I was taped passed out to the hood of a car."

I remembered when Katy and I brought baby Eilif to visit our relatives in the city of Bodø and my Norwegian cousin Ole Magnus was decked out head to toe in red with a giant "DRÆGNI" written on the front of his *russ* overalls. I asked his mother, Rigmor, "Is that so when he passes out they know where to bring him?"

Rigmor laughed nervously and Magne Drægni responded, "We don't know what Ole Magnus will do, and he won't tell us anyway. It's better that way because I really shouldn't know."

The *russ* crawled through downtown on kneepads as a prank and held up traffic when crossing at stoplights. I asked Inger to please shed some light on this bizarre Norwegian phenomenon. She told me a *russ* committee is elected at each school by the students, and it determines what tricks the *russ* have to perform between May 1 and May 17 to earn a *rupe* (ropelike tassel). "We would do very stupid things like go into the garage where they keep the police cars, and when they weren't looking, try to clean the whole car with a toothbrush. I was thrown out of the police station for that one," admitted Inger.

I hadn't seen many police cars in Norway—mostly fire trucks blaring through town. When asked about this, Inger told me, "That's because we Norwegians very much follow the law when it's necessary. Maybe that's why another thing we did was try to kiss a policeman and then you earn a—how is it in English—a tassel?" I'd also heard that the *russ* get a new knot in their tassel for each night they spend awake. Don't forget that during this entire time they should be studying since these are the three weeks prior to their final exams.

I was more confused than ever, so my classmate Vigdis tried to help me understand. "Some *russ* have drinking rules to get each other drunk. When I was *russ,* some of us cut a square meter of grass with a toenail clipper, and others sat in a tree for thirty-three hours, thirty-three minutes, and thirty-three seconds. Then they got a tassel."

I scratched my head at this obsessive-compulsive cleaning, but Vigdis didn't give up. She told me how the *russ* "get a little meaner to the younger students. The *russ* often enter into the first-year [high school] classes and squirt them with water—when the teacher's not there of course."

Vigdis explained that the orange *russ* are those graduating from junior high. "You're dead if you meet a red *russ* and you're orange," she warned, adding, "They could take your hat and cut your rope [that held the tassel]."

"People let the *russ* do anything they want for a week," Vigdis explained. "Sometimes it's a problem, like in Oslo where some students bought a red bus for some million kroner and then drove around town with very loud music and interrupted people who were working. The police stopped them many times."

"Did they ticket them?" I asked.

"Oh no, the police told them to turn down the music. They never give them fines."

"So being *russ* is like a protective state," I said, "just as long as you don't actually hurt anyone else."

"That's true, the police never do anything to you when you're *russ*," Vigdis replied.

I soon realized the danger of the *russ*'s carte blanche when Vigdis told me, "The one horrible case that was in all the newspapers was when *russ* tied up the hands of a younger student and then tied a section of that rope to the bumper of a car and he had to keep up with the car. When he fell down, they just dragged him."

This actually sounds criminal, I thought. Vigdis shrugged at the lack of common sense of the new *russ*.

Beginning with May Day, I saw more and more *russ* celebrating in the streets with joyous singing and loud horns. A group of ten *russ* who wanted to be seen were hanging out in the middle of a grassy traffic circle and occasionally would venture into the onslaught of cars to direct the mass of oncoming cars with a loud whistle. The drivers humored the *russ* and followed the confusing directions. After mocking traffic cops became tedious, the whole gang piled inside a red van that pulled up to carry the moveable feast elsewhere.

As the days went by, the poor *russ* looked more and more haggard in their red outfits that evaded washing machines since the poor teenagers rarely slept in order to keep up with their friends. Outside of the train station, I saw a female *russ* dragging a leash with the end tied to a foot-long mackerel. The wide-eyed tourists at the station watched as the brave *russ* swung the fish around until the body popped off of the head of the poor fish. The *russ* didn't even notice and kept dragging the fish head around on the leash.

The fun of this two-and-a-half-week party became more forced with each day, and I felt sorry for the *russ* who obviously wanted to rest. The *russ* with the fish head sat on the curb and nodded off. Her friends woke her up, and they pushed a shopping cart full of empty beer bottles with three large trash bags full of bottles and cans on top. At least they recycle, I thought, as they trudged home to sleep.

No, I definitely didn't want Eilif to be *russ,* but he was clearly intrigued by these bizarre hazing rituals. He asked for more information from Jan's son Henrik, who was about to become *russ* the following year. Henrik explained that the *russ* were like royalty at his high school and blacklisted everyone younger than them.

"The school administration doesn't like the blacklist,"

Henrik told Eilif. "Then all the *russ* sit at a special round table in the cafeteria because they think they're special."

Eilif asks, "Does everyone know which table?"

"Oh yeah, it's the only round table," Henrik responded. "When someone who isn't *russ* sat there, they threw a watermelon at him."

"A watermelon?"

"Yeah, that wasn't such a good idea," Henrik replied, "but it was pretty funny when the *russ* wrapped all the chairs in the dining hall in plastic wrap." Now Henrik is planning how to do them one better when he is *russ* next year.

All this talk of hazing reminded me of the tour we had just taken down on the Bryggen in Bergen of the old Hanseatic houses from around the 1350s, when the fourteen-year-old apprentices withstood dangerous hazing to be part of the group. The guide, Kay, told us how these teenagers underwent terrible "rituals where they were stripped naked, keel hauled, beaten by others, and held upside down over smoky fires. Then they were the kitchen helpers and cooks. Would you really want a fourteen-year-old as a cook?"

"Especially after you treat them like that," I muttered. What would stop them from poisoning the bullies?

"Nowadays they don't do so much hazing," Kay added, referring to both apprentices and students, "mostly scavenger hunts and drinking from bar to bar."

Not everyone is so thrilled that the *russ* madness continues. Anne from Oslo told me, "*Russ* has to end. There have been too many assaults."

Magne told me that "*russ* used to start the last day of April and finish after the seventeenth of May, but now they start earlier and earlier." The authorities have cracked down on *russ* since we lived in Norway fifteen years ago. "Now they can't buy a van or a vehicle and paint it red since too many got hurt. Now they have to pull a trailer in the parade."

Despite these peculiar and sometimes dangerous traditions, the Norwegian education system is excellent and free. If Norwegian students survive their *russ* experience, they can choose to attend one year of *folkehøgskole*. The vision for these folk high schools came from Nicolai Grundtvig, a Dane, in the 1830s as a reaction against the rigid established educational system. He developed a hands-on discovery model with no exams or grades. The idea encouraged a democratic dialogue between teacher and student with no one above the other.

The idea of college in Scandinavia is even better. I read an article in the Italian daily newspaper *Corriere della Sera* explaining that Danish university students not only get a free college education but are actually paid to attend college. I showed it to some Norwegian friends, who said that it's the same in Norway. Denmark spends about 1 percent of GDP, or about 3.3 billion Euros, a year on higher education and up to 7.9 percent of GDP on all levels of education. "From outside, this seems like public assistance, but it's the opposite: an incentive to leave home early and succeed on one's own," the article said. Danish students get about nine hundred dollars per month for living expenses. "The fundamental purpose of this assistance is social mobility. No capable students should be forced to give up on their education because they don't have the means to pay for it," according to David Elmegaard Jensen, an official who works for the Danish government agency that distributes money to students.

Odd Lovoll, who taught at the University of Oslo for nine years, confirmed that "education is free, but they accept anyone who wants to try for a PhD. I don't think it's good since many don't make it." Still, these people try for a better education. The investment pays off since Norway has the highest number of young people who graduate from college, followed by the United States. The difference is the debt.

I had tried to explain student debt to my relative Rigmor, but she didn't understand since it seemed like such a foreign concept, like charging kids to go to public high school. Her son Ole Magnus then complained about his Norwegian student debt.

"What?" I responded. "I thought that tuition was paid in Norway."

"Oh it is," he said and explained how the Norwegian State Educational Loan Fund, known as Lånekassen, gives loans to students at little to no interest to help with room and board. In certain cases, the loans can be completely forgiven.

I heard my friend Magne lament about Norwegian universities: "We didn't have to pay any tuition, but we did have to buy books!" Considering student debt in the United States, I couldn't believe he was actually complaining about the low cost of books compared to tuition.

I explained to Joffe and Runa that I was worried Eilif would be straddled with debt after college. Runa was shocked, "Are you really so cruel in the United States? These young people will have no future if they have debt from school, have no health insurance, and cannot get a house or do anything. What future will they have?"

The Culture House

BEFORE OUR TRIP, I had reached out to various venues to see if they'd like me to give a reading from my previous books. I had already given scores of presentations around the Midwest, even paid sometimes, and I thought I could do the same in Norway. I offered to present for free since we'd be there anyway. My friend Knut suggested Litteraturhuset in Oslo. I wrote to the director to offer to read there and to help promote the event. Instead, their booking manager sent me a price list, indicating that she expected me to pay up to a thousand dollars to be given the opportunity.

I was dumbfounded and wrote back explaining that this would only allow the rich to be writers as a sort of hobby. Besides, the abysmal pay of writing books would bankrupt any aspiring writer who has to "pay to play." Isn't this a form of payola? She didn't understand, and I chalked it up to a cultural chasm between our countries. I'd heard that Norwegian art, music, and literature are highly funded, but the grants only go to artists "approved" by those in the appropriate government agency.

Once Eilif and I arrived in Trondheim, I asked our host Joffe about how the arts work there. He is part philosopher, part musician, and part artist working as a "bureaucrat" (apparently not a negative term in Norway), who advocates for all forms of art, from classical painting to gritty underground obscenity. Part of his job is to determine how art is actually a valuable cultural asset.

I explained the Litteraturhuset incident to him, and he was disgusted but not surprised. "How do we explain that art has value beyond just money?" Joffe wondered. "Does art need to be monetized and commodified to be valuable? Wait, money itself now has cultural capital." Thanks to Joffe, Litteraturhuset in Trondheim was thrilled to have a reading, just for literature's sake. I had to know someone in the system.

Most towns have a *kulturhus*, a culture house supported by federal funds. I learned that they serve as a mini-museum, community center, and dance hall and are sometimes connected to the community pool, library, café, cinema, and sports center. I loved the idea of taxpayer money going to support the arts but worried that the Ministry of Culture had to give its stamp of approval. "We've come to accept that the arts, theater, and literature should all be supported by the government," Hans Erik in Oslo told me.

Because of this, everyone has an opinion about the arts since their taxes support it. For example, the new boxy Munch Museum in Oslo is the object of either scorn or admiration as a nearly windowless mini-skyscraper. "Why always gray?" Inger asked. "The building looks like stacked-up traffic barriers."

Her husband, Knut, worried that "the most important art in Norway and perhaps one of the most important collections in Europe could go up in smoke since these skyscrapers are like chimneys."

Hans Erik approved of the radical modern design, countering, "Does everything just have to be a wooden box in Norway?"

His wife, Anne, simply thought it was ugly and cold.

Knut works as a curator at Oslo's National Gallery, which has a brand-new government-funded building. He told me that his new office only allows each person one and half meters of bookshelf space, "since everything can be found online," according to his bosses.

"What about art?" I asked. "Can't that just be found online too?"

He joked, "Yes, what's the point of museums when we can all just stare at art on our phones?"

Thinking about government-supported "culture," I remembered a festival Katy and I had stumbled on fifteen years ago. Considering Norway only has five million people, the government must support these festivals. Katy and I had traveled up the Sognefjord with baby Eilif to the tiny town of Balestrand the same day that the nationally known jazz festival Balejazz was getting rolling.

On our way there, we'd passed by a Viking statue of Fridtjof the Intrepid, donated by the German Kaiser Wilhelm II around 1913 as his idea of what the culture of the area should be. Here in Balestrand he erected a statue to the Viking king Bele next to another version of what Norwegian culture should be, this time according to an English woman from Leeds. The quaint "English Church of St. Olav" with menacing wooden gargoyles peering from the edge of the roof was built to resemble her vision of a Norwegian stave church.

This backdrop along the fjord seemed the most unlikely venue for jazz. Families with children in strollers came from the wooden houses around town to gather on the green grass for a concert.

I was curious to see how Norwegians would view the decidedly American tradition of jazz. The first band, "Gentle Groove," had a repeating light funk bass with bland syncopated guitar and drums to produce a Muzak version of Ornette Coleman. No one except Katy shared my view, though, and the lawn was full of kids and parents happily dancing.

The next band cleared out the dancers except for tough-looking teenage boys and their fathers. Four guys with long hair and matching "Gluecifer" shirts broke into nearly perfect Led Zeppelin covers. The cranked-up volume bounced off the nearby buildings, and some of the families—including us—took a walk from the free "jazz" concert.

Pushing Eilif in his stroller, Katy and I looked around the few shops for a restaurant. Since Balejazz in early May makes for the biggest tourist week, apart from the high summer season, Kvikne's Bistro was full of people drinking beer. I asked the waitress if we could see a menu, but she responded, "We don't serve food during the jazz festival. We wouldn't be able to handle the volume of people."

I immediately thought about what our friend Knut had exaggerated about the Sognefjord: "No one lives there really." As famous as the area is for its beauty, the population is very small and is surely doubled or tripled when the tourists arrive.

The only restaurant we found open was the Sognefjord Steakhouse, and my mouth watered with the thought of a big juicy steak with baked potato and Texas toast. A large sign on the door announced this was a "Jazz-Free Zone."

Judging by the music we'd heard so far, perhaps we'd actually hear jazz inside. Instead, the speakers played muffled black metal music with distorted guitars shredding the fretboard behind falsetto singers screeching about life's pain. The steakhouse was deserted except for a couple necking in a secluded booth and the vicious-looking bartender perched behind the enormous wooden slab of a bar. His black T-shirt had the sleeves torn off to reveal his serpentine tattoos on his bulging triceps as he carefully dried wine glasses. When we sat at a table rather than the bar, he sighed loudly and threw down the tea towel in annoyance over the interruption. He trudged over to our table but didn't say a word.

"Can we see a menu?" I asked.

"No . . . we only have pizza," he finally responded.

"So you're not a steakhouse?" I asked.

"Well, we are, but we only have pizza now."

"What kind?" Katy asked.

"Pepperoni."

"And?" I asked.

"Only pepperoni," the bartender grumbled as he threateningly put his hands on his hips. A chain wrapped around his waist as a belt rattled in rhythm with the death metal piped in over our heads.

Both Katy and I knew that the overpriced meal would be a heated up Grandiosa frozen pizza, the most popular meal in Norway.

"That's OK. Thanks anyway," Katy replied, breaking the tension.

"Goodbye! Have fun at Balejazz!" the bartender said, suddenly chipper, relieved that he didn't have to work.

Katy and I looked at each other surprised and wondered if he'd just put on a tough act for us. We left the restaurant interested to see what the next act of Norwegian versions of American/British music would bring. After Gluecifer's metal act came four guys dressed in flannel shirts and cowboy hats playing a cover of Lynyrd Skynyrd's "Sweet Home Alabama."

Work Happiness and Living Off the System

AFTER MY READING at Litteraturhuset in Trondheim, I caught up with some of my classmates from the university. Vigdis had worked as a journalist for eight years at a newspaper in the town of Steinkjer, until it began to downsize. "The newspaper was shrinking, but they can't just fire people."

"Really?" I asked, since that happens all the time in the United States; I know many journalists who had lost their writing jobs in Minnesota. Instead, Vigdis's newspaper offered her a big severance payment. She took the buyout to spend time with her kids and start her own marketing and consulting business that used her journalism skills. She could afford to do this since the Norwegian government provides all their health care and her husband was working too.

Our friend Inger asked, "Is it true that many people are just one paycheck away from having no money? It must be very scary to live in the United States since if your child gets sick you don't know if you can afford health care." She couldn't believe that if people go to the hospital, even with health insurance, they could risk bankruptcy.

Work didn't seem to be such a source of stress here, which they summed up in one word: *arbeidsglede,* or "work happiness." My friend Jarle told me, "No one has to have two to three jobs as you do in America. We need to pay people a living wage even if they work in fast food. Minimum wage is at least twenty dollars an hour for an adult, depending on experience." Despite Norway's comparatively high wages, the World Bank reported that companies have an easier time doing business in Norway than in the United States because the workers are generally highly educated and health care is covered by the government.

I'd heard that only tiny Luxembourg has a higher per capita earnings GDP than Norway. "In 1984 Norway became the most productive country of the world," economist Tor Dahl told me. "Singapore is more productive than Norway now and perhaps China is as well. Singapore had a better model with forced vacations, education . . ."

Caleb Crain in the *New Yorker* recommended the Nordic model and suggested that the United States would "be better off with redistributive programs that are universal— parental leave, national health care—rather than targeted. Benefits available to everyone help people without making them feel like charity cases." The Scandinavian governments support their workers "through wage subsidies, retraining sabbaticals, and temporary public jobs." The cost is very high though. "True," writes Crain, "Denmark's spending on its labor policies has at times risen to as high as 4.5 per cent of its GDP, more than the share America spends on defense."

Incredibly, Norwegians have been working 23 percent fewer hours a year since the oil boom. My classmates from Trondheim worked hard at their jobs but had a comfortable work-life balance. "If you work your ass to death, you're not doing anyone any favors," Tor told me. "If work is 'play' for you, you'll be unstoppable."

A biennial study called "How's Life?" of well-being in thirty-five Organisation for Economic Co-operation and Development countries found that only 3 percent of Norwegians work more than fifty hours a week, and they generally have decent work schedule flexibility.

"We have shorter workdays," Inger told me, "but we are just as effective as others. At my library, [the staff] take responsibility at their level because they know what to do."

"There are always freeloaders, though," her husband, Knut, added.

That's when I learned about the new Norwegian word of the year, *å nave*, which means to live off the Norwegian welfare system and comes from the abbreviation NAV for the organization Nye Arbeids og Velferdsetaten, or New Labor and Welfare Administration. Whenever I asked Norwegian friends about this, they all chimed in. "A *naver* is someone who doesn't do anything," an acquaintance who works for Equinor told me. "There aren't many and it's ugly when you don't want to work. As long as you're searching, you can be on it, but NAV will find you a position."

She added that Norwegian employers generally cannot fire employees at will. "To get sacked, it can take months. First you must have lots of meetings." She seemed to be saying that workers can slack off and keep their job but that the bureaucracy will eventually catch up.

Since Magne had lived in Minnesota for many years, he saw how his fellow Norwegians had become "soft." He observed, "Younger people in Norway haven't seen bad times. The recession in 2008 lasted two to three weeks. People were going crazy when the unemployment rate *increased* to 3 percent."

Magne talked about how he knew of Norwegians who preferred not to work and collect unemployment rather than work at McDonald's. "If they have everything provided, why should they work?" Magne asked me. "I think that they are a little spoiled—no, a lot spoiled! People need goals and ambition, but I think they say, 'why bother?'"

Jan told me during our stay in Bergen that he had visited Minnesota a few years before. A taxi driver picked him up at the airport and was excited that Jan was from Norway. "I heard you don't have to work in Norway!"

"No, that's not really true," Jan responded, explaining that the government gives unemployed Norwegians barely enough to survive.

The taxi driver chose not to hear and repeated, "So it's true, you don't have to work in Norway!"

Not only do Norwegians work fewer hours (and are more productive) than most of the world, but they also retire much earlier, at an average age of 63.5 years old. Kari, a professor of education in Bergen, told me about traveling to the United States with her son: "We had an elderly waitress in Georgia who had to work to survive. That would never happen in Norway since they would have retired by then."

Despite the generous pensions from the Norwegian government, senior citizens who go to live in a nursing home must give up 85 percent of their pension, according to my friend Jarle.

Our host Joffe can't wait to retire and never look at a computer or cell phone again. "I'm reading *The Internet Must Die* and can't wait to just read books."

Blind Rage and the Weekend Drinking Binge

FIFTEEN YEARS AGO, when Katy's water broke, we took a taxi from Trondheim to the hospital in Orkanger an hour away. Today, Joffe and Runa took the day off work to drive Eilif and me to the town of his birth. Years ago on that taxi ride, the road wandered along the shore of the fjords. Now tunnels have halved the driving time and made the view non-existent.

While in the car, Eilif suddenly blurted out, "I heard that the Vikings drank so much aquavit that they were brave enough to go into battle."

I searched for context for this out-of-the-blue comment, but I suppose we had seen Munkholmen and talked about St. Olaf.

Joffe didn't miss a beat. "Actually, Eilif, that's a myth that the Vikings were all drunk before battle, since hard liquor wasn't made here until the 1500s, well after the Viking period."

Runa added, "Instead, the Vikings took mushrooms to make themselves crazy to become berserkers for battle."

They explained that the blind rage, *berserkergang,* of Vikings was practically a trance from hallucinogenic mushrooms. Joffe told Eilif that psilocybin mushrooms grow everywhere in Norway.

"Wait!" said Eilif, looking out the car window in search of mushrooms, "so the Vikings were on 'shrooms?"

Our conversation digressed to other mind-altering substances. I tried to steer the conversation away and instead mentioned the Scandinavian fascination with *snus,* or snuff. More people pop some *snus* between their lips and gums in Norway than smoke. While the European Union has banned *snus,* Swedes and Norwegians love it. Overall, 12 percent of Norwegians use *snus,* and Jan told me that about 20 percent of young people do. I'd even heard people say, *"Fint som snus,"* or "fine as snuff," which means "right as rain" or very healthy, which it definitely is not.

Norwegians also indulge in strong coffee, more than sixteen pounds of coffee per person each year to get through the dark winters. This beats every other country except for Finland. To offset all that caffeine, the Finns also drink far more alcohol than the Norwegians, more than twelve liters per person per year.

Alcohol is easily the biggest problem of all. By the early 1800s, Norwegians had so many stills for homemade aquavit that there was one for every ninety people. "During World War II, there was no liquor, no smoking, no sugar, no meat—that all went to the Germans," my friend Tor had told me, "but Norwegians were the healthiest they've ever been despite the war."

Runa said that drinking is not everywhere in Norway. "In Sogn, some of the older people there only drink alcohol once a year. It's very conservative and religious."

All alcohol sales go through the municipal liquor stores, Vinmonopolet, or "The Wine Monopoly," so the profits support the government. These government liquor stores buy in bulk, and sommeliers choose the wine, so I've never bought bad wine in Norway. To pay for the true cost of the alcohol on society, the Norwegian government adds about thirty-four dollars of tax per liter of hard alcohol. Of course, this leads to massive amounts of smuggling over the border, mostly by Russians and Eastern Europeans, I'm told. For example, at just one bridge crossing, Norwegian customs confiscated 20,000 liters of hard alcohol and 140,000 liters of beer in just six months. Despite this big haul, they estimate catching only between 5 and 10 percent of smuggled alcohol. A rough estimate of the amount of beer smuggled per year is between six and twelve million liters. I'd heard that the Norwegians go to Sweden; the Swedes go to Denmark; the Danes go to Germany; and the Germans go to Poland.

I then realized that the three liters of Minnesotan gin that I brought in my suitcase as gifts to Joffe, Jan, and others constituted smuggling. I could easily have been fined $175 at the airport. They thanked me profusely for the gifts, and I realized why when I saw that the cheapest beer at the supermarket was eight dollars a bottle.

A friend from Oslo, Anne, told me that she was nabbed for bringing in forty bottles of wine from Sweden for her wedding. She was "so embarrassed" that she now has a "criminal record" but told me the story:

> My dad was a pilot and used to bring in bottles that he would hide in secret compartments in the plane. He was with me in Sweden and thought I was trying to bring back too much. "Oh no," I said, "it'll be

fine." Then the border patrol stopped our car and let all the others pass. I think they have police in civilian clothes watching in the Swedish stores. They pulled us over and asked if we had anything extra today. "Oh yes!" I broke down crying and confessed everything. They were very polite and didn't care about the extra meat—only ten kilos per person is allowed—and let my dad and I keep our three bottles. Nowadays you can keep six bottles. I had the choice of a five thousand kroner fine or five days in jail. Nowadays, this wouldn't go on my criminal record, but it's still on there and we had to explain the situation when we adopted our son.

When I was a student in Trondheim, I remembered hearing about *helgefylla,* or the "weekend drinking binge," which I suppose happens on college campuses around the United States as well. One of my classmates, Juri, couldn't come to a barbecue because he had to clean up from the previous night's party with his rugby team. "We must bring three hundred bottles to return to the grocery store," he told me. "Twenty drank all this beer!"

"I didn't have any," an Italian student Serena said.

"Yes, that's right. Some people didn't drink any, so there was more for us," Juri said. "Thank you very much." Then he told us how his rugby team stripped on the pitch after each game. Serena asked how this last game of the season went. Rather than respond with words at the barbecue, he and his teammates stripped all over again and ran around outside.

My Norwegian classmates were often painfully reserved and polite, but then I'd hear stories about the weekend binges. "Norwegians don't know how to behave," Tor Dahl told me. "They have to have a drink before they can talk."

This reminded me of the saying my Norwegian professor told me, "Don't open your mouth to show how dumb you are," which is similar to what Mark Twain supposedly said: "Better to keep your mouth shut and appear stupid than to open it and remove all doubt." Apparently, this rule applies in Norway except when you're drunk. Then you can blame it on the liquor. Perhaps this isn't different from many other places, but I was just hoping for better in case Eilif wants to move here for school.

I had told friends in northern Italy about Eilif considering studying in Norway for a year since Norwegians are so "happy." Valentina was shocked: "The Norwegians are all crazy—all of them!" She said that all that the Norwegians did was drink.

I pointed out that Italians often sip wine at lunch and dinner and that many people in Norway (and the United States) will drink milk instead.

"That's worse!" she said, appalled.

Another Italian friend said it was disgusting that we drink milk at meals, as if we're just grown-up babies.

"I had a friend from Italy who went to Norway and said they all just look down and never talk to each other," Valentina said. "Then they drink until they can't stand up—especially on the weekend. The police come around in the dark—it's always dark there—and have to help these drunk zombies home so they don't freeze to death. How is that happy?" She said that Eilif should go to Italy, where he'll be happy.

"That's old Norway," Tor Dahl reacted after I told him about Valentina's views. "Norway used to be terrible, but people who are serious about sport can't drink the way Finns do."

I knew that Norwegians sometimes harbored harsh thoughts about Swedes, but the Finns?

"Finns are drinking more than ever—like the Russians," Tor explained. "If you are on a bus and sit next to a woman, she'll move. The only thing that loosens them up besides drinking is the tango. That's how they get married."

Perhaps after the new World Happiness Report came out declaring Finns the happiest in the world, Norwegians felt they had to defend their second- or third-place finish. For example, a Norwegian woman I met, Gro, explained, "I've heard that the Finns are happier now, but maybe that's because they know how to drink."

Jan Brøgger in Bergen also refuted this idea that Norwegians drink so much and said that drinking too much was more of a Finnish habit. "We Norwegians drink the second least of anyone in Europe, right after Albania, which is mostly Muslim." I looked it up, and he was right, but Italy was essentially tied with Norway and Finland wasn't that much more.

The drinking age in Norway is eighteen for beer and twenty for hard liquor. "Young people in Norway drink less, use fewer drugs than before," Kari, the professor in Bergen, told me and then whispered, "We sometimes think it's a bit too perfect."

I'd heard a story, though, from the bus driver Petter from Trondheim, who told me about a Norwegian exchange student who lived with a family in the United States for a year. "At eleven and a half months, the family went out of town for the weekend, and the Norwegian student had a party at the house. She cleaned everything, but the next day the father found a beer cap under the couch. He went crazy! They talked about how she had lost their trust and she needed to leave immediately—after a year together! Everyone was crying and it was just awful. Is this how it is in the United States?"

Folketrygden

The People's Insurance

WE ENTERED THE SMALL CITY of Orkanger where Eilif was born and immediately spotted a replica *stavkirke*, or stave church, that we'd seen before, but never here. Before bringing Eilif to Norway, I had taken our family to Norwegian sites around the Midwest, specifically to "Little Norway" near Blue Mounds, Wisconsin. I snapped a photo of Eilif in front of this replica stave church, which was originally built in Orkanger and then shipped to America along with a replica Viking ship to represent Norway at the 1893 World's Columbian Exposition in Chicago. After the festival, the church became a cinema and then moved to Little Norway, Wisconsin, a historical Norwegian farmstead. Little Norway shut down in 2012.

As we planned our trip to Orkanger, I discovered that after 122 years, the stave church "went home" to Orkanger. A group of Norwegians traveled to Wisconsin to dismantle the *stavkirke* and lovingly restored it as a little bit of the Midwest in Norway—just as Eilif was born in Orkanger, grew up in the Midwest, and has now returned.

We drove to the Orkdal Sykehus, the hospital where Katy and I came for her pregnancy checkups. She had begun to refer to her pregnant self as "we," so I was always out-voted two to one in anything we did. Being pregnant opened doors. This worked to our advantage since we were nervous about having our first child in a foreign country. We had flown to Norway with no health insurance because the woman at the office for international students in Trond-heim told me over the phone, "You should just come over anyway."

I explained that we couldn't pay for the birth.

"Oh, you Americans!" she interrupted. "You have such strange problems. That's not an issue here in Norway."

We soon found out she was exactly right. We had to wait for the *trygdekontor,* or insurance office, to open in September because "when you arrive here in July, the sun will be out all day. It's been a long, dark winter, so everyone will be at their cabins in the mountains or at the seaside." Apparently the sunlight trumps everything in Norway.

If Katy had been working in Norway before the birth, she would have received forty-two weeks off from work at full pay or fifty-two weeks at 80 percent of her salary, paid for by the government, not the employer. Since she hadn't worked, they gave us a cool five thousand dollars to help raise our baby, plus the government covered all the medical expenses. Not bad.

I assumed that the reason the United States hasn't adopted socialized medicine like Norway is the cost. "You spend 20 percent of your GDP on health care for shitty results!" Jan Brøgger corrected me. "We spend 10 percent and it's great."

To check this out, I spoke with the economist Tor Dahl, who had slightly different numbers but the same result: "Health care in Norway consumes 9 percent of GDP; the

United States consumes 17 percent of GDP, and half of it is wasted." Millions still aren't even covered by health insurance in the United States. According to the Organisation for Economic Co-operation and Development, Norway is one of the highest spenders on health care, and their costs are still significantly less than the United States. Denmark, for example, has excellent health care that only costs 7 percent of GDP.

I would think business leaders in the United States would want health care covered by the government to avoid paying it themselves. My employer and I pay almost twenty thousand dollars per year for my health insurance—and I still have a high deductible of fifty-eight hundred dollars for our family plus all the co-pays, dental expenses, and so forth. If we are truly a country of entrepreneurs, don't we want our workforce to be mobile? So many independent contractors, artists, and musicians could flourish. An article in the *Washington Post* in 2020 explained that the United States pays a trillion dollars a year more on health care than the next highest country (Switzerland). The United States ends up paying for this health care anyway, but just not in an efficient way. The writer argued that every American family essentially pays an eight-thousand-dollar poll tax whether they have health care or not.

"If you are sick in Scandinavia, you can get money," a Swede working in Geilo told me. "No one is left out; we take care of our people."

"If you are sick here, all surgery is free, all hospitals free, and you can choose your own doctor," Jarle, the teacher from Oslo, said. "You need to contribute for some medication, but mostly expensive medication is all free." He said that doctors sometimes have a twenty-five-dollar consultation fee that people complain about, but there are no big waiting lists for elective operations, as many people in the United States claim. "There is a guarantee from the government that cancer patients will be treated within twenty-one days."

The historian Odd Lovoll didn't paint quite such a glowing picture about the Norwegian health-care system: "After seventy, the hospitals won't treat you for certain things, and after eighty they won't treat you for others. Many people go to England because they have more specialists." Then he admitted, "Of course, the Norwegian system is better because it's free and treats everyone." When they say "free," however, this means that taxes pay for it.

I learned that everyone in Norway has a right to a pension since the Norwegian Parliament passed a law in 1967 to establish *folketrygden,* or "people's insurance," even if a citizen has never worked. Odd talked about how sometimes the government even pays for people to be sent on vacation. "Yes, you can be sent to Syden [the South] for more sun, especially if you live in a place like Finnmark [in northern Norway]. Most people pay their own way, of course." He told me how his father was sent twice under medical orders to the mud baths in Yugoslavia for a restful cure.

I imagined what it would have been like if my Swedish American grandmother had had this kind of treatment available in Minnesota. I remembered her telling me that when she was in her forties, "I was so sick of my teeth. One day, I just went into the dentist and I had him take them all out."

"Really?" I asked, as she showed off her false teeth.

"Yup, he pulled every single one. It was the best thing I ever did."

On the other hand, I heard that in Norway all dental care is covered until twenty years of age.

As Katy and I were preparing to leave Norway to go home to the United States with baby Eilif, we had a pregnancy scare and wondered how it would look if she had come to Norway pregnant and returned home pregnant again. We considered perhaps staying longer for help with the next baby. After all, the government provided nearly free day care and deposited about $150 each month into our bank account to help raise Eilif.

The Norwegian government kept depositing money into our account even after we moved back to the United States. I had to compose a letter to them: "Please Norwegian government, stop sending us all this money." I sometimes regret sending that letter, especially after doing the calculations: $150 x 12 months x 18 years = $32,400.

Instead, we came back to the United States, and I heard that the benefits of having a child in Norway have increased in an attempt to avoid a negative birth rate. Eventually we had two more children in Minnesota with no extra government help. The deductible on our insurance that we had to cover was five thousand dollars—exactly the opposite of Norway and a ten-thousand-dollar difference.

Aliens Were Here

DRIVING ON THE WINDING ROADS near the hilly fjords of Orkanger made me think of all the mythical creatures of Norwegian folktales hiding out just beyond our sight. This reminded me of my visit to Iceland the year before and hearing how plans to lay new roads over the island were scuttled because of "little people" living there. My Icelandic guide Börkur was serious when he said that you didn't want to upset the elves' habitat or they'd make your life terrible.

I asked Norwegian friends if they have similar beliefs based on the old folktales that told of trolls on the top of the mountains throwing down rocks. I'd heard that mountain peaks are actually trolls' teeth and giant rock formations are petrified trolls who stayed out too long and saw the sun. Jan explained that Norway is not superstitious like Iceland, but still Christmas is all about *nisser,* or pixies, since Santa Claus is one of them. "At home, we have our *nisser,* the house pixies," Jan explained. "If you are ever missing something or suddenly find candy, it's probably because of them. If you are good to them, they will bring you gifts at Christmas."

He told me about the *huldrer,* beautiful women who live in the mountains but have long tails so are clearly not human. "We have a neighbor who swears he saw a *huldra* up in the mountains in Nordfjord," Jan said. "You know there are young women who go up to live in *hytter* in the high pastures, and they stay with the animals up there."

I thought about all the woodland creatures frolicking about and all the strange stories of unexplained events in the mountains. When we'd lived here, Katy and I had traveled just southeast of where we were in Orkanger to investigate rumors of UFOs.

I had written to one of the researchers, Erling, who picked up Katy and me at the bus stop in the tiny town of Ålen. We were weaving around switchbacks on a treacherous mountain road, when Erling stopped the car on a precipice and pointed. "It started down in the valley, and someone saw it moving up the hill there. The lights are yellow, many white, some are blue, very few green, also different types of colors. It's been so bright that part of the valley is illuminated at night."

Erling was describing the almost regular unexplained light spectacle in this land of the northern lights. "It's not the aurora borealis," he cautioned. "The lights are down in the valley, and there are no houses there. Even the Norwegian Air Force has seen something and can't explain it. When a plane comes, the lights go away but often come back afterward."

"I try to avoid the term 'UFO' because most people immediately think of it as nonsense and then no scientists want a part," explained Erling, who was a lecturer in computer science at Østfold College. "We try to use the term 'Hessdalen Phenomenon' after the name of the valley." Even so, Erling had helped the café in town add a "UFO Senter" with numerous photos of the mysterious lights, video footage of UFOs, and paintings of big-eyed aliens.

As Erling kept driving up the mountain to the UFO

observation point, his cell phone rang. One hand steered his Suzuki jeep up the steep incline while the other held his phone to his ear. His face turned somber from the news. He hung up and said, "That was the police. There's a missing person in the area, so I have to stop and talk with them because we have many observers scattered around this area."

After a stop at a ranger station on the top of the mountain, Erling returned to the car. He saw no relation between the possibly abducted person and the mysterious lights. "The missing man is mentally unstable, so they'll use a plane first to see if they can see him in the valley." Then he added, "Many of the police have seen the lights too."

"I've been working on 'Project Hessdalen' for more than twenty years, and the phenomenon has slowly diminished. There's no good theory to explain it, but nothing can really cover all of the things that happen here. Some think it's because this is one of the areas of Norway with lots of sulphur and copper, but Røros has copper too and there are no lights up there." Erling obviously had his theories, but he seemed to want us to make our own conclusions.

"People weren't aware of the lights before, but if you know they exist you start seeing it too and realize that your eyes aren't playing tricks on you. Sometimes we're not sure if we actually see the flashes though. That is when we check our machines." Just then, Erling turned off the road, put the Suzuki into four-wheel drive, and revved up a field to a little automatic monitoring station.

He opened the closet-sized metal building with antennas, satellite dishes, and cameras blossoming out of the roof. Inside, gadgets and monitors filled the walls with names like "Inspire," a magnetograph low-frequency electromagnetic detector made by NASA. "We control all this through the internet," Erling said proudly. "Whenever anything happens, the cameras will photograph it." Erling showed me a stack of photos taken by a spectral camera of the phenomenon and boasted that his video had even appeared on the Discovery Channel.

Next stop was a little Norwegian *hytte* mountain cabin filled with students ranging from twenty to forty years old in Hessdalen to study the phenomenon. A flying saucer jungle gym stood outside, and *"Aliens var her"* (Aliens were here) was spray-painted on the wall. Inside, a map of *stjernehimmelen* (the starry sky) was tacked on the wall above a coffee table loaded with Geiger counters and "electromagnetic sensors."

Some students were still sacked out in sleeping bags on the floor with their rucksacks as pillows after spending the night on a "UFO safari" in the hills, while others were cooking up "Yum-Yum" ramen noodles. "There was this rising light and many people got very excited," one of the students told me. "We all started taking photos, but it was just the moon rising with the clouds in front of it."

"Later on, though," added another student, "we saw small blinks and a light pole slowly rise up the hill. That was real."

"The biggest observation was when we stood up quickly and got lots of little stars going on—about fifty or sixty of them," teased a student with a perfect southern twang acquired from a year in Alabama.

The other students laughed but weren't fazed by his skepticism. One of them said, "It's very exciting to sit there and to take measurements. We took photos of sparkling lights down in the valley . . ."

". . . and then we stopped drinking the moonshine," the "southerner" added.

At that point, Erling interrupted because it was time to catch our bus home. In the car ride back over the mountain, he speculated, "It's too early to say what causes this light phenomena. I could make all sorts of silly theories, but we'll wait till we get better info." He scoffed, "Some people in Hessdalen claim they haven't seen the lights. They just don't want to be connected with it."

I asked Erling if he'd ever seen any unexplained phenomena during the day. "Yes." Just lights? He hesitated and chose his words carefully, perhaps for fear of losing credibility. "No, I've seen metallic-like objects and something that was cigar shaped." Then he added, "I choose to focus on the lights, though, because it has been a proven phenomenon."

Sakte

Slow

AFTER WE SAID GOODBYE to Joffe and Runa in Trondheim, Eilif and I headed north on a little train that wiggles ten hours up beyond the Arctic Circle to Bodø, the farthest north that trains go. Here the sun doesn't even pretend to set. Day and night lose their meaning. This concept that time no longer has significance and that the past, present, and future are all here at the same time is summed up in the book that both Eilif and I were reading at the time, *Naïve. Super,* by Trondheim's own Erlend Loe. The book is a funny Norwegian *Catcher in the Rye* and perfect for Eilif's teenage weariness with the world.

Tourist brochures boast that the Bergen-Oslo train line is the "World's Most Beautiful Train Ride," but I would argue that Oslo to Trondheim beats it and Trondheim to Bodø is better still. The view out our window was a picture-perfect scene of snowcapped mountains with few trees, cuddly baby lambs playing in the lush mountain meadows with mountain flowers, and patches of snow with waterfalls cascading off cliffs. Blueberry bushes sprouted next to moss-covered rocks (old trolls, they say), and white paper birch rooted in nearly impossible cliffs—Dr. Seuss would be proud. The train entered a cloud, and we didn't see any sign of life for a half hour. When we finally did see a house, it was a grass-roofed *hytte* with kids out front waving to the train from their idyllic pasture.

The *hytter,* or cabins, are cherished by Norwegians, and laws protect the historic ones. "To fix up an old house, you must do it *innenfor ramen,* 'in the frame,' or within the rules, but it's very expensive, so many people just let the house tear down itself," according to Magne.

A recent law went into effect to prohibit new buildings within one hundred meters of the coast. I wondered how anyone could build in a place like the Lusterfjord, where there often aren't even one hundred meters between the shoreline and the vertical cliffs. Magne explained that some people avoid these laws by just building a temporary plastic structure, or *spikertelt* ("nails tent"), around an RV since it's so much cheaper and not subject to all the regulations.

The idea of a classic wooden *hytte* with a wooden loft (*hems*) and even wooden utensils is fixed in the Norwegian psyche. *Å gå på hytta,* or "to go to the cabin," means to get away from it all and back to one's roots—the more isolated the better. "Joffe always wants to go to the *hytte* and is fine being so remote, but I want to be where the people are," Runa told us.

Joffe wanted to be away from Wi-Fi and just read his books and the newspaper in a remote *hytte* in his ancestors' village of Urnes in Sogn. He saw how Norway, like the rest of the world, had become obsessed with the internet: "Social media has become a tsunami of irrelevance. It's been devastating to journalism because they only care about the clicks. People only read the headlines." He wanted to unplug to get peace of mind in a secluded cabin.

"We used to go to Sogn more often, but it's such a lonely place," Runa added. "I don't know how people do it. It's beautiful, but not an easy place to live."

Norwegian television taps into this love of the *hytte* with shows like *Sommerhytta* in which contestants must fix up their *hytte* for the summer. Another *hytte* program features the most remote places that people live, like on a desolate island or on a cliff only accessible with ropes and ladders. Certain cottages are so secluded that the mail is delivered by snowmobile.

This love of being away from it all reminded me of another student who came to Norway at the same time as Katy and I did. She hailed from Fargo, North Dakota, and was going to Tromsø, another eight hours north past Bodø. "What are you doing?" her friends back home asked. "You're going to the middle of nowhere!" She told me, "I'd look at them and say, 'Do you think that Fargo is in the middle of it all?'"

The northern Norwegians are fiercely proud of being from above the Arctic Circle. Tor told me that "90 percent of northern Norwegians go back to where they came from after coming south for their education." Looking out the window, I could see the appeal, but they had to be hardy.

I scanned the forests for moose since a couple on the train said they had just seen one next to a river. Norway has so many moose that they talk about bizarre instances of *elg-skrekk,* or "moose terror." According to the daily newspaper *Aftenposten,* a moose broke into grocery stores, a moose attacked clotheslines it didn't like, and moose get drunk on fermented fruit and stagger into towns (not unlike university students on Saturday night).

One confused moose wandered into Oslo after hearing shots in the forest during hunting season. The moose got caught in a gated courtyard of apartment buildings on Rosenhoffgata after walking into Carl Berner's Place, one of the busiest intersections of town. The article said the police had already given up on tranquilizing moose that venture into cities. Instead, police sharpshooters got their rifles ready, but in this case they had to wait an hour before their ammunition was approved. The moose's terrorizing of the town lasted three hours, and then a crane was needed to move the dead animal because it weighed so much. In the end, at least, someone probably had a good meal.

Our friend Knut raved about moose meat. "You should really stop at a little hamburger stand a couple of hours north of Oslo," he told us. I think he was referring to the red-and-white mushroom house next to a moose statue 140 miles north of Oslo that we'd seen. "There they make mooseburgers that taste like good American hamburgers." To have a real beef hamburger in Norway, we have to eat moose?

Looking out the window, I felt like I'd gone back in time to a world I didn't know still existed. As I ate a delicious waffle at the snack bar thinking about the fact that I was the farthest I'd ever been from home, the cashier brought me back to earth. "You are from Minnesota? I have friends in Stillwater."

Despite these vast distances in this long, narrow land, Norway is strangely united. In an attempt to bring together the country, there are no long-distance calls within its borders; they are all cheaper local calls. Roads, tunnels, bridges, train lines, and ferries connect even the most remote places so everyone doesn't move to the cities. For safety and likely to conserve gasoline, the busiest roads often have a speed limit of only 80 kilometers (50 miles) per hour.

NRK TV has tapped into this Norwegian desire to slow

down with Sakte-TV, or "Slow TV," which features lengthy programs that are perplexing to inattentive audiences used to the quick cuts of modern TV to keep their interest. Imagine watching eighteen hours of salmon starting to spawn or a twelve-hour program on log burning. NRK had a hit when it mounted a camera on the train from Bergen to Oslo for the seven-hour trip. As Eilif and I traveled on the train to Bodø shooting blurry photos out the window, I understood why Norwegians would want this beauty to enter their living room.

NRK's most popular television show of all time featured a six-day show that aired nonstop with a camera mounted on the bow of the MS *Nordnorge* Hurtigruten ship. The ship sailed from Bergen all the way to Kirkenes on the Russian border, and people set up bonfires and parties along the route to be on national TV. The 134-hour show aired in Denmark as well to two hundred thousand loyal viewers; Norwegians mocked the Danes with their flat country for having "mountain envy."

The Slow TV movement parallels the Italian Slow Food movement as a reaction to unhealthy American fast food, corporate farming, and immoral feedlots. On the train, we passed by Levanger, a city that has declared itself a Sakte By, or "Slow City," to encourage local food production and as a protest against corporate consumer culture. This designation might not be so appealing to everyone. For example, my cousin visited her relatives on a quiet island near Stavanger. I asked if she would want to move there. "Umm . . . not really," she hesitated and then whispered, "You know, it's just kind of boring."

This desire for silence and serenity obviously takes a certain person. Nevertheless, Sakte-TV lives on. Knut told me about a five-hour show on knitting a sweater, beginning with shearing a sheep. "These shows unite the country in a strange way," he said and told me about a lengthy show of reindeer herds moving. "I don't know of anyone who actually watched it."

The Dark Side

JUST BEFORE ARRIVING IN BODØ, the train passed through the town of Mørkved, or "the dark side," which wasn't dark at all since the sun was poking through the clouds. We realized we hadn't seen darkness for more than a week. We were just three weeks away from the summer solstice.

The last time I had taken this train trip between Trondheim and Bodø was in February fifteen years ago, when the train's electricity went out. We spent ten hours in complete darkness with a fussy newborn. Now the sun wouldn't let up, dipping briefly below the horizon around 3:00 a.m. only to pop up an hour later.

Even at 3:00 a.m., though, the pinkish-yellow light of sunset would keep streetlights from turning on. I remembered hearing a neighbor in Trondheim mowing his lawn at 1:00 a.m., and others decided that midnight was a perfect time for a barbecue. We heard workers outside of Runa and Joffe's house at 3:30 a.m. in neon-lime jackets. Do the words "night" and "day" still apply?

Døgn is the Norwegian term for a twenty-four-hour day, whether it's day or night since the endless sun or darkness makes day and night irrelevant. When Katy and I had just arrived in Norway and had asked our landlord, Arne, in Trondheim when we would see darkness, he replied, "In July, the sun goes down about nine o'clock, I think." He didn't know.

At 10:00 p.m., the sun started to set.

At 11:00 p.m., it hadn't quite gone down.

At 2:30 a.m., I woke up, and the sun still wouldn't stay down.

"From November to around April we don't have light," Arne told us.

His wife interrupted, "*Nei,* we start to have light in March."

In Bodø, where the Drægni relatives live, they experience the *polarnatt,* or "polar night," the months-long night above the Arctic Circle. With this lengthy *mørketid,* or "dark time," I understand why everyone is out worshiping the sun in May.

"In the summer, I feel there is so much to get done!" Joffe told us. "Time slows down in the winter, and that's OK. I love the darkness."

His wife, Runa, didn't agree, especially since her family had moved from sunny India. "How do people live in this lonesome country?" she asked. I told her how the Hurtigruten ship that Eilif and I took stopped in the cities of Kristiansund and Ålesund on the way to Trondheim and hardly anyone was on the streets—and this was May with full sunlight. Imagine January!

"I have more problems now with the darkness than I used to," Runa added. "I need to go south to get some sun."

This was echoed by others when I asked Norwegian friends how they could be so happy in a dark country. "Happy? Norwegians aren't happier than anyone else," Odd told me. "I heard of a truck driver from Oslo who said that he'd give up a little of this happiness if he could live in Italy."

Not everyone is thrilled when the *lystid,* or "light time," of spring arrives. Our guide in Bergen, Kay, complained, "Those darn birds! They're so loud and keep me awake all night. I can't wait for the winter so we can sleep!"

The term for "spring depression" is *vårdepresjon* and can also translate, ironically, as "our depression." Kay told me that the suicide rate actually goes up in the spring when people see how happy everyone else is. I point out that this is the opposite of *skadefryd,* or schadenfreude, the malicious joy one feels at others' misfortune. Perhaps this is part of the reason Norwegians try not to show off. For example, if you have a fancy sports car, you'll just make others feel bad, so why buy one?

This ties into the distinctly Scandinavian idea of *Janteloven,* or Jante's Law. The Norwegian Danish author Aksel Sandemose wrote about this hidden code of conduct in his satire about a fictional small-minded Scandinavian town. The ten rules proclaimed, "You shall not believe that you are wiser than others. You shall not believe that anyone cares about you." And other soul-crushing commandments.

Even if Sandemose mocked this humility as promoting conformity, Norwegian mothers today tell their children, "Remember your *Janteloven!*" In other words, don't get cocky or show off.

When Katy and I returned to the Midwest after our year in Norway, we saw remnants of this Scandinavian stoicism everywhere. When I'd wear a nice suit and tie, everyone asked, "Who are you trying to impress?" Wearing flashy clothes or flaunting wealth is in extraordinary bad taste, as are bragging, making noise, and whining. Everyone should be content with what they have because it can always get worse, right?

Complaining is simply not acceptable because it won't do anyone any good. Even in hospitals, some surgeons have noticed that Norwegian Americans require less anesthesia than others. In Finland, 80 percent of women giving birth refuse epidurals, whereas 90 percent of American women ask for these painkillers. The Finnish word *sisu* sums up this concept and means resilience, "guts, grit, determination," or "stubbornness beyond reason."

In fact, I read that "anger in Finland is a bigger taboo than sex." Ask yourself, is it OK to get angry in the Midwest? Do you have to apologize afterward? In Mediterranean countries like Italy, anger is passion and passion is love.

In the Midwest, being quiet and shy is considered humble. Or as the Finnish joke goes, "How do you know if the Finn on the elevator with you is outgoing? When he's looking at your shoes instead of his own."

The humor is dry wit that is often self-deprecating rather than showy puns or sight gags. Making a scene is frowned upon.

Most outsiders view this Nordic stoicism as a fatal character flaw that makes for insensitive, uncaring, and even boring people, but Scandinavians, unconsciously or not, regard this seeming indifference as being reliable, solid, and, well, downright good.

Keeping your cool is the ultimate in cool, but never show that you think you're cool. Sure, the Italians are the best dressed, have the fastest cars, are the most outgoing, but how do they do with thirty-below windchill?

"We don't want to overdo it," as my dad says. This extends to taking halves—and halves of halves—of the remaining food on the table to not appear too greedy. Never take the last little bit.

Minnesota style is often "anti-style" as well. Never show off your wealth. Shyness is OK, or as Norwegian journalist Odd Eidem wrote, "Norwegians are seldom spontaneous before they have thought about it a bit."

Katy and I had observed this shyness around Trondheim. In the Solsiden shopping center on the edge of downtown, a man had set up a little demonstration table to sell new cell phones, but he was too shy to approach people. We watched him try to make eye contact with shoppers, but everyone was too polite and respectful to stare. Also, they probably just didn't want another cell phone offer.

When we went to the local film club in a small theater to see the noir classic *Double Indemnity* with fast-talking, witty dialogue, a young man got in front of the small crowd to introduce the movie. He looked out at the people, and his speech became broken, he stuttered, and he could barely get the words out. When he finished, everyone clapped for his brave effort.

We'd also heard that because of *Janteloven,* Norwegians are very slow to invite anyone to their house. Because of this, we often said to the few Norwegians we had met, "We really should have you over sometime." We meant, of course, maybe sometime this year if we ever get around to it. Maybe. Then, however, they would call us a couple of days later and ask, "When shall we come over to dinner? Is Monday OK? If not, Tuesday works as well."

Although it was great to make friends, we became careful not to make vague invitations unless we meant it. We found Norwegians we met remarkably social, despite their reputation as go-it-alone, rugged individualists who shunned chitchat in favor of being by themselves. In fact, I was supposed to give a presentation in Milan about

Scandinavia with Swedish Italian director Erik Gandini, who planned to talk about the grim situation of elderly Swedes living and dying alone.

"Ugh, that's a little much," my Italian friend Anna said.

Somehow, though, these grim details fascinate many of us, even if we don't want to admit it. Perhaps this is why the Nordic crime novels are so popular.

I worried about Eilif's reaction to these bleak events, but seeing Edvard Grieg's strange tomb in Bergen didn't faze him either. Grieg was less than five feet tall and suffered from a collapsed lung at age sixteen due to tuberculosis. Upon his death he was put in a cave down below his house with his wife.

"That's just what they do in Norway," Eilif joked. "They shove your body into a cliff."

Perhaps Grieg's charming wooden house full of instruments overlooking the water made this more palatable since Eilif assumed that most musicians live in gorgeous places like this. Of course, we were there in the summertime with gentle light warming our cheeks.

We'd heard that tourists now are streaming into northern Norway in the winter to see the darkness. The coastal steamer Hurtigruten offers northern lights tours in the middle of winter and promises visitors that they'll see the aurora borealis or their money back. I loved seeing the northern lights in January but didn't know if enduring the winter was worth it, considering that all the darkness is just like being locked in a closet.

The writer Garrison Keillor went to the northern Norwegian city of Tromsø in the middle of winter. "I want to see the northern lights," he told me. When he returned, he said he had caught a terrible cold.

"How was it?" I asked, hoping for some humorous revelation on the long winter.

"It was dark," he responded.

When we finally arrived in Bodø after passing Mørkved, our relatives Magne and Rigmor Drægni picked us up at the train station. It was still daylight, of course, so why go to sleep? The *midnattsol*, or "midnight sun," kept shining, and guests stopped by that evening around 9:00 p.m. Just like Grieg, Eilif was ready for music. He pulled out his guitar and played a mini-concert, and everyone clapped along.

Strangely, I felt like I needed the night. While the sun gave us energy to keep going, we were ready for the darkness. After several hours of the party, Rigmor said, "I'm not tired, but I suppose we should sleep at some point."

Ut på tur, aldri sur

Out on a Walk, Never Cross

NORTHERN NORWAY seems like it's on the edge of the world. I realize why people from the rest of Norway, which is already so dramatic, venture farther north to be closer to nature. The teacher Jarle introduced me to the term *jord-nær*, literally "earth near," and the importance of this earthiness, which is also your past: "You need to be connected to the soil. My parents were hard workers, fishermen and farmers. Happiness is about accepting who you are: your family history and what your past is. Don't deny where you are from and what your parents have done to get you where you are. For kids, it's possible to change who you are, but don't forget your past."

The connection to the past and family is often linked to the *hytte*, or cabin, which has often been passed down through generations. With a population of just over five million, Norway has four hundred thousand of these cabins. Time off, presumably to spend in nature and with family, is codified in law, with a guaranteed minimum of three weeks of vacation. Often these cabins are the ancestral home, but the earth in Norway is notoriously bad for farming. Only 2.8

percent of the land in the country is farmable, compared to 85 percent of the land in Iowa.

Many of the city-dwelling Norwegians we knew couldn't wait to get out into the country for an "outdoor life," or *friluftsliv*, literally "free-air life." This need for fresh air extends to the indoors as well with the term *inneklimat*, or "inside climate," which seems to be a constant topic of conversation. Anna, the Norwegian law student I met who was living in the Twin Cities, said, "It's terrible here [in Minneapolis] with the screens on the windows in the summer because I can't get enough breeze into my apartment. In Norway we don't have many screens because we want the fresh air." In fact, our apartment in Trondheim had no *myggnett*—"bug nets" or screens—on the windows. The gentle winds would waft through our apartment, and I imagined being able to sleep under the stars out in the woods, if we didn't have a baby, of course.

Norwegian happiness seems directly related to time spent in the wilderness. "We are outdoor people," Gro from Bergen told me. "We are happy because we are close to nature." Being out in the woods is considered a right in both Norway and Sweden, enshrined in a law called *allemannsretten*, or "everyone's right" to roam free. No one absolutely owns the land since anyone can come and camp there for a night. "You just need to clean up in the end and not sleep on the farmer's doorstep," Jarle from Oslo told me. "Wherever you go, no one should see any trace that you've been there."

Jan in Bergen clarified, "You can camp anywhere just as long as you're one hundred meters away from someone's house. Norway is mostly uninhabited, rocky, mossy forest, so why not?"

If you don't want to camp and don't own a family *hytte*,

you can "register with the Norwegian tourist association and then have a self-service *hytte* with the key hanging above the door waiting for you," according to Jarle Nesvaag. The Norwegian Trekking Association (DNT) was formed in 1868 with just sixteen cabins in the high plains of Jotunheim and Hardanger, but now hikers can rent a *hytte* all over the country.

Norwegian explorers are, of course, some of the bravest to ever risk the elements in extreme weather. I remembered when at a party at Knut's apartment when he still lived in Trondheim that he, Joffe, and other friends discussed how Fridtjof Nansen and his sidekick Hjalmar Johansen went to the North Pole aboard their "brilliant" boat, the *Fram* (Forward), with its hull that would be pushed up from the pack ice rather than crushed. When the *Fram* could no longer move, they started toward the pole with kayaks and sleds and made it within 272 miles of the pole. Nansen and Johansen had to sleep in the same sleeping bag for weeks. Only then did Nansen say, "Johansen, I think that it is OK if we now use the informal form [of speech]."

"There has been a lot of speculation about what went on in that sleeping bag!" one of the guys at the party said. He explained that when Roald Amundsen went to the South Pole, he refused to have the explorers sleep in the same bag even though it made sense to preserve any heat they had.

"I can't believe that the British would try to go with horses or on foot. They didn't even use snowshoes or skis!"

"However, it does make for a much better story," Joffe added, "rather than these Norwegians who simply make it there and back."

The other friend replied, "That's when Amundsen answered about the English going to the pole, 'Let the British do what they do best: die.' Amundsen did have a way with words." They didn't mention that the English accused Amundsen of tricking Captain Robert Falcon Scott by changing the Norwegian expedition to the South Pole at the last minute.

We talked about other explorers, and I mentioned that now the United States is talking about setting up a station on the moon.

"Well, who owns the moon?"

"America must because the American flag is there," Knut said sarcastically.

"Well, if that's the case," Joffe said, "then Antarctica is Norwegian because Amundsen was the first to plant a flag there!"

Although I think of Norwegians as cooperative community builders, Tor Dahl corrected me: "Norwegians are the most competitive people on earth—except for maybe the Chinese." For such a small country, Norway is remarkable not only in its exploration but also in its accomplishment of winning more gold medals in the winter Olympics than any other country, and by far.

It's no coincidence that Amundsen and Nansen knew that skiing was the best way of traveling over snow since the word "ski" comes from Old Norse. The earliest evidence of skis is in Norway, and early runestones reveal carvings of Ullr, the Norse god of skiing. The famous story of two Birkebeiners skiing over a mountain with a baby king has spawned lengthy cross-country ski races.

When Katy and I visited Lillehammer, we heard of a mountain biking version of the fifty-four-kilometer Birkebeiner race up and down the mountainous ski runs. People got up extra early to watch them ride—and perhaps fall?—down the slopes.

This lust for danger is summed up in the insanity of the monstrous ski jumps across Norway. "All kids try ski jumping at some point," Magne told me. "We start at about three years old. You pile snow together and start at two to three meters high. Little by little you start jumping houses and get up to ninety meters."

When I was little, we made two-foot-high jumps for skis and sleds, but jumping houses? Then my dad told me that his dad jumped off of his garage roof when he was young. No wonder my dad waited until now to tell me!

I'd seen the Granåsen ski jump in Trondheim and visited the gigantic 197-foot-high Holmenkollen in Oslo. If this isn't high enough, new jumps are even higher, and daredevils risk their necks for "ski flying," reaching up to one hundred kilometers per hour. This need for speed and cold danger could be summed up by figure skater Sonja Henie, who talked about the somehow pleasurable icy winds slapping her face while skating, skiing, and sledding as "winter drunk."

I didn't need this extreme danger or cold but was impressed by how nearly everyone would ski and bike. When we lived in Trondheim, the *trikk* (tram) hauled people from the center of town twenty minutes up to the ski trails out of town. During the oil crisis of 1975, King Olav V famously sent a signal that he was one with the commoners when he took the tram in Oslo to go skiing.

Of course, the winter is mostly dark, so the trails have special sensory lights that click on when skiers pass by. I found the dark a good reason to hibernate, but our landlord, Arne, told us, "We like to go skiing after work or school." He then patted his stomach. "I must go with my bike to the center or ski twice a week because I like food very much!"

Katy and I tried to ski when we lived in Norway, but having Eilif as a newborn stopped us, until the ski shop rigged me up with a *pulk*, or baby sled with rigid poles attached to my waist—as if cross-country skiing wasn't enough exercise already.

I looked longingly at other skiers being pulled by dogs. When we returned to Minnesota, I saw skiers practicing this Norwegian sport of *skikjøring* but learned that it also allows the skier to be pulled by a horse or motorized vehicle. When I was growing up near Lake Minnetonka, we would "water ski" on snow and ice behind a car with a rope attached to the bumper. We thought we were being stupidly dangerous, but who knew that this was a trendy sport?

Just as the "Extreme Sports" store in mountainous Voss offers more ways for athletes to risk their necks, another Norwegian wrote a best-selling book about the seemingly tedious task of wood stacking. The common thread, though, is a love of the outdoors.

Many Norwegians told me, "*Det finnes ikke dårlig vær, bare dårlige klær*" (There is no such thing as bad weather, only bad clothes). In other words, you have no excuse not to go outside. A rainy day in the fjords only heightened the drama when the sun poked through. Kids in damp Bergen typically trudge around in raincoats, pants, and Wellington rubber boots. Norwegians often have their skis ready to go as soon as the snow falls.

When Katy and I lived in Norway, people would only greet us out in the countryside, as though the city was stifling them. As with all cities in Norway, the wilderness is nearby and easily accessible by public transportation. Most

Norwegians I spoke with listed nature as an important aspect of their happiness. Now as Eilif and I traveled into northern Norway, I understood why the natural beauty is so important to the Norwegian national character.

I remember that as a kid I hated being forced to go out on nature walks, but as an adult I love it. Now I'm trying to convince my lazy teenager Eilif to go on a forced march in the wilderness. Joffe recommended being prepared for grumpy kids with the "Norwegian rucksack" packed for an adventure, containing a sweater, a swimsuit, an umbrella, a *matpakke* (food pack of *smørbrød,* or sandwiches, and a Kvikk Lunsj, a "quick lunch" candy bar), and a thermos of coffee or cocoa. Joffe talked about getting his girls out on hikes no matter what the weather and preaching the Norwegian saying: "*Ut på tur, aldri sur*" (Out on a walk, never cross).

Frisk som en fisk

Fresh as a Fish

TODAY WAS THE KIND OF DAY where we had to decide what we were made of. Magne and Rigmor wanted to take us fishing at the Saltstraumen maelstrom, a watery vortex between the ocean and a fjord where the tide pushes more than one hundred billion gallons of water back and forth every six hours through a narrow channel.

The weather was gloomy and wet, so they would understand if we didn't want to go. Eilif was content just staying inside and relaxing on the couch strumming his guitar; I wouldn't hear of it. "When else in our lives are we ever going to go fishing at Saltstraumen?" I asked. Eilif grudgingly put down the guitar.

"Well, we can't just stay inside all day," Rigmor agreed. "We must go out!" She had knit matching blue-and-white sweaters for Eilif and me out of beautifully soft wool—not like the scratchy Dale sweaters. To layer over our *lusekofte* sweaters, Magne equipped us with rubberized raincoats and pants since the temperature showed 8 degrees Celsius with a stiff wind. Even so, we saw people around Bodø in similar outfits strolling in the rain undeterred. The neighbor kids were jumping on a trampoline and playing badminton despite the wind and sleet. I remembered what Petter, the bus driver in Trondheim, had told me, "If you wait for good weather, you'll never be happy."

Magne loaded up his fishing tackle and told us, "I took off my snow tires with the *pygge* (studs) today because I hope it will truly be spring." It was June 1.

Next to his garage—and nearly every garage in Norway—stood a bin filled with sand "because of all the *slaps*," I'm told. I love the sound of Norwegian weather words: *slaps* is snow and ice together (slush, but not so watery); *sludd* is sleet; and a snowflake is *snøflugg*.

Our friend Runa in Trondheim told me that "many Norwegians aren't such talkative people and are hard to get to know," but you can always make small talk about the weather. I've found I can carry on an entire conversation without understanding a word. I get things going with a provocative statement like "*Det er så kaldt i dag!*" (It's so cold today). The response is usually a bit of disbelief that I'm really so wimpy followed by a whole weather report and an analysis about how this year is nothing compared to, say, fifteen years ago. And, of course, there's back in the 1920s. Is it global climate change, greenhouse effect? I can't follow any of this, but it was certainly fun to hear the dramatic dialogue from normally quiet folks.

This idea of not complaining no matter how bad the weather brought me back to an ice story that our Italian friend Marcella had told us when she lived in Trondheim at the same time as we did. She lived up a hill, so she could get some sunlight and have a great view of the city and the fjord. One day, she walked home carrying two big bags of groceries and looked up her long, steep driveway ahead. Water flowed over two centimeters of ice that covered the

driveway, making a sheer Slip 'N' Slide. "I thought if I went nice and slowly it would be fine," she told Katy and me. "I took a few steps and fell on my face. For some reason, I tried to protect the food and slid back down the hill. I had a cut on my lip and a huge bruise on my cheek." She had to use her cell phone to call her boyfriend inside the house to come down the driveway and pick her up in the car. "Even the Norwegians who live upstairs couldn't climb up the hill, so it doesn't only happen to Italians!" she said. Later that evening, she went to a formal party. "I started half dreaming while at the party and realized that I had a concussion."

No wonder the weather is so important; it can mean life or death—or at least grave injury. When I found documents of the correspondence between my great-grandfather who came to Minnesota and his relatives back in Luster, writing about the weather was just as important as news of dead relatives.

I noticed on the front page of the daily newspaper *VG* that weather warnings are prominently displayed, along with the banner headline "Vitamin D makes you smart" with glossy photos of a salmon fillet and bottles of Möllers cod liver oil. When Eilif was less than a week old, the doctors made us feed him cod liver oil with little eye droppers, which he would then spit up all over his one-piece pajamas. Our Italian friend Marcella was amazed that Norwegians make their kids take cod liver oil: "Well, Mussolini did the same thing. His torturers fed dissidents a whole bottle of castor or cod liver oil until they had diarrhea for a week."

Since four-fifths of Norwegians live within a dozen miles of salt water, the newspaper announcing that fish is good for you sounded a bit like studies sponsored by the wine lobby that reveal drinking two glasses of merlot every day assures excellent health or the dairy council's study that a half pound of cheese a day is the best source of calcium. Even so, I've been brainwashed to believe in the powers of *tran* and have continued to give our kids the slippery cod liver oil. The Norwegian nurses convinced us that if we neglected to give them their daily dose, our children would have rickets, develop bad eyesight, and just be generally a bit slow mentally—and who wants dumb kids?

Today, though, rather than give spoonsful of stinky fish oil to Eilif, we went to catch fresh fish. Magne and Rigmor drove us out of town through Mørkved and some new tunnels, dark passages they didn't particularly like but that they admitted made traveling faster. Coming out of the black underground was like emerging out of the long lightless winter into eternal sunshine, although today the cold, wet *sludd* kept our happiness in check.

We drove along the coast past tents of German campers

braving the elements, and then we saw it: a sleek white bridge over the swirling whirlpool of the Saltstraumen, the strongest tidal current in the world. Magne hooked up three long rods with wormlike rubber lures, while Rigmor watched us walk down the slippery rocks to the churning water.

Magne had the timing just right, and we only had about a half hour for the height of fishing. I showed Eilif how to pull back the rod and let out the line at the same time he flicked it forward. His first cast he lost his lure pulling it back. Fish by the dozens popped their hungry heads up above the furious foaming surface looking for a bite; we just had to cast out far enough, but we were busy trying to rig up another lure for Eilif.

He had a beautiful cast but wound it back so quickly that the hook snagged a rock and the line snapped. Eilif took off his shoes and was ready to wade out into the roiling water with the swift undercurrent that has brought down ships for centuries. "What are you doing?" I demanded and stood in his way. "You want to walk into the maelstrom?"

"It's hooked just six feet from the shore. I'll be fine," Eilif said. I realized he was embarrassed that he'd lost another lure, but I assured him that we'd rather lose a million lures than him.

Magne deftly put on another lure from his collection, and we all hit the jackpot. We reeled in fish as fast as we could cast, but the tidal flow was almost over. Eilif admired his sixteen-inch shiny fish, proud of the perfect little creature that had come in from the open ocean.

Magne unsheathed his knife, sliced under the fish's gills, and ripped the fish's head off as Eilif stood shocked. Rigmor pulled the guts out with her hands and threw the intestines up for squawking seagulls eager to get in on the slaughter. Eilif was disgusted, a bit sad he lost his beloved fish, but impressed at the ruthlessness of it all.

Rigmor rinsed the fillets in the salt water to boil at home later for a delicious dinner. Magne was pleased with the catch. He smiled at Eilif, patted him on the back, and praised him: *"Du er en sterk Drægni!"*—You're a strong Dregni!

Naked and Safe

THE EVENING NEWS above the Arctic Circle in Bodø announced yet another mass shooting in the United States. Magne and Rigmor looked to me for an explanation, and of course I had none. "Should Eilif really stay in the United States?" Rigmor asked, apparently thinking he should remain in northern Norway where it's safe.

"I'm kind of down on America right now," Eilif said rolling out of bed at 11:00 a.m. We loaded up our backpacks in the car to go to the airport for the last leg of our trip in Norway, Oslo, and I explained how his grandmother, my mom, hadn't wanted us to be Americans with a target on our back and had wanted to sew Canadian flags on our backpacks. I refused since we shouldn't hide who we are. "We need to be good ambassadors for our country, right?" I said, not entirely convinced.

Eilif clearly felt that Norway was much more liberated and pointed out that the drinking age is even eighteen.

I countered by pointing out that the driving age is only sixteen in the United States. Magne and Rigmor were surprised and a bit relieved that Eilif wasn't driving yet.

Eilif said we should let him get his driver's permit now that he's fifteen. He's upset that Katy and I want him to be older before he can drive. "Why not? I'm responsible!"

We bid Magne and Rigmor farewell at the airport and prepared to board our flight to Oslo. In the Bodø airport, the airline officials didn't even check our IDs. I tried to show them our passports, but they were uninterested.

I rarely saw armed police, or many police at all. Murder is thankfully rare. All of Norway has only about twenty-five murders a year, whereas sleepy St. Paul alone had thirty murders last year.

I wondered if Rigmor was right that Eilif should stay in Norway. Many Norwegian friends pointed out that women can walk alone at night here and not feel afraid. I read in the newspaper that a burglar was caught breaking into a house by the owner, an older woman. She called the cops when she saw him coming in through the bathroom window. By the time the police arrived an hour later, they found the thief to be well fed.

I remembered too when Katy and I traveled with her American friend Margaret on the Hurtigruten coastal steamer to visit her relatives on the Lofoten Islands. In the ship's cafeteria, Margaret found a wallet left on one of the tables. She reached to pick it up to bring it to the cashier in case anyone claimed it. When she touched it, an older Norwegian woman a couple of tables down shooed her away from the wallet as if Margaret was stealing. Margaret tried to explain, but they couldn't understand her English and just nodded suspiciously at the shady American. At another nearby table, a different vigilante do-gooder watched the wallet as well and shook her head at Margaret.

The idea of safety here goes beyond just crime. "More people have enough and more than enough. They feel economically safe," said Kari, the professor of education, whom I met on a plane. "It's not just the money. You can get sick without having to worry. We don't have to have the daily struggle of how is it going to be tomorrow." She then told me about her son who went to live in the United States. "He's taken on American values, which I'm not sure I agree with. . . . For example, you have the homeless in the United States; we don't have that in Norway."

I heard a similar sentiment from twenty-four-year-old Stine in Geilo: "You know there's a lot of terror; the rest of Europe is not so safe. The government has been watching. A lot of us are living in good conditions. The rich aren't really rich and the poor aren't really poor. It's really good for young people. We don't have really big debt." She said that conditions are very safe, especially in rural Norway. "Norwegians are perhaps too naive and think always the best of people. People don't lock their cars—or houses—in Geilo."

The one notable exception to all this feel-good security is Anders Breivik's murderous attack in 2011. Reading about his trial, I was shocked that Breivik was allowed to spout his insidious hatred to the courtroom and the world. If he had done this in the United States, the courts would not have given him the forum to promote his manifesto. Kari said, "Even when he spoke, we were not afraid." Amazingly, the Norwegians didn't try to suppress his message but wanted to expose it for its absurdity.

After this massacre, Norway didn't militarize with police on every corner. Even when Munch's *The Scream* was stolen—twice!—armed guards with submachine guns were not summoned to the museum to protect it.

Our plane landed in Oslo, and this big city felt like much more of a metropolis than any other city in Norway. We couldn't afford a hotel, and the apartment of our friends Knut and Inger was far too small. Their friends Hans Erik,

Anne, and their adopted eleven-year-old son, Henrik, agreed to host us for a few days.

I told them how no one checked our passport, and they said, "Why should they?" Hans Erik said he was appalled by the surveillance culture in China when they went to pick up Henrik. "They had cameras everywhere and a room with screens that monitored our every move."

"I don't think they had them in our hotel room," Anne said, but then after thinking about it admitted, "I guess I don't know . . ."

"Probably not, but I can't be sure," Hans Erik said.

"To get a visa into the United States you need to give your Twitter handle and Facebook username," Inger pointed out. "Is it so different?"

I told them I was concerned that everyone used their debit cards all the time in Norway, which can be easily traced. Inger was surprised that we wouldn't trust our banks, but I don't know why I would trust them any more than my government.

I explained that I was shocked when "I tried to pay for a beer at a hotel in Trondheim, and they wouldn't accept cash. I'd never heard of that. That seemed like Big Brother to me."

Inger said this was common and countered, "I can't believe you still use checks in the United States."

I explained that I usually have three forms of payment. "I'll use a check if I don't have cash and don't want to use my credit card."

"Oh, we don't use credit cards so much," Inger said. Apparently most of the cards in Norway are debit cards.

I remembered Joffe in Trondheim talking about wanting to use a debit card when he had traveled to Greece, but nearly all transactions there are in cash. "We tried to rent an apartment in Corfu, but they wanted to be paid all in cash." He said this shows a distrust in the system, which he also saw in Berlin. "Most people there use cash since they don't want the government to be able to trace them."

The next morning, I was finally able to get Eilif out of bed before 11:00 a.m., and we piled on the bus that would take us from their suburban house into Oslo. I fumbled in my pocket for the right change to pay the bus fare as the driver waited impatiently. Apparently most people use a bus card that a high-tech scanner reads, but I asked the driver to repeat the price. "Just get in. Don't worry about it," he said kindly since he was impatient with these backward Americans. From then on, Eilif figured out the money and had the map on his phone of where we needed to go.

I suddenly felt aged and that the tables had turned. I couldn't keep up with the times and my spacy teenager could without even thinking. I had become my dad, and I thought about the trip that we made through Scandinavia when I was sixteen. I remembered being pleasantly scandalized by the hippy heaven in Copenhagen and all the nude sunbathers in Sweden. Now it was my turn to be the conservative one with my son.

We hopped off the tram at Frogner Park to admire the statues of Gustav Vigeland. I pointed out the statue of an angry boy, "Spitfire," that had inspired Katy and me to get through Eilif's colicky phase when we lived in Trondheim. Eilif wasn't so interested but noticed all of the other statues. "Ha! They're all naked!" he said delighted.

The sculptures span a lifetime from birth to death, and he was clearly moved. He loved the freedom and the cosmopolitan atmosphere of Oslo. Maybe he would fit in here after all.

A Night at the Nobel

I POINTED OUT THE RÅDHUS, Oslo's city hall, to Eilif and tried to tell him how important this building is, but I couldn't muster any enthusiasm. Frankly, it's rather ugly and reminds me of cold Soviet constructivist buildings that try to convince the citizens of how noble Russia's fearless leaders were. Eilif was unimpressed, and it didn't help that a classic amusement park, Christiania Tivoli, had been torn down to build this dark brick government building—which at least has a fantastic gilded astronomical clock on the facade and beautiful murals inside.

The building was closed, however, so Eilif couldn't see the paintings. Most of the artworks promote labor and industry and the notion that hard work made Norway great; Eilif wouldn't be impressed anyway. I finally got a small reaction when I mentioned that this is where the Nobel Peace Prize is awarded.

Alfred Nobel, a Swede, willed that all of his awards would be given in Stockholm except for one: the peace prize. In 1900, when Nobel established the awards, Norway was united with Sweden, and some speculate that he respected the mediation of international disputes by the Storting (Norwegian Parliament).

"We live in a peaceful country, but what is 'peaceful' in this world now?" Gro from Bergen asked.

Jan was very worried about Russia since NATO has been weakened. "Russia could easily march through Finland and Sweden since they are not part of NATO. Norway is impossible to defend with all its coastline." Jan said that Norway was in big trouble if the United States pulled out of NATO.

Eilif said that he thought the United States was already out of NATO. I couldn't tell if he was joking when he said, "Poor Russia, they are always the bad guys. They're not so bad." Inger was left speechless.

I heard on the NRK evening news about the discovery of a beluga whale off the coast of Ingøya island armed with some sort of radio transmitter attached to a belt that read "Property of St. Petersburg." Russia denied everything; Norwegians assumed it was a top secret spy whale. The friendly beluga wouldn't leave and even retrieved an iPhone that a woman dropped while trying to take a photo. The animal's disposition led experts to conclude it was probably an escaped therapy whale. Even so, during the Cold War, Russia and the United States had tried to train dolphins and belugas to find mines and warn of approaching submarines.

Russian submarines dive far deeper than any others but sometimes get stuck in Norwegian waters in the Barents Sea. Magne told me about one particularly daunting time when a Russian submarine ventured into a Norwegian fjord. "It was all the talk in the newspapers for many days. Is it war? What will we do? Then suddenly nothing. They let it go since they didn't want to make it a bigger issue."

I asked if Norway still has mandatory military service, since I was worried that if Eilif became a dual citizen he could be drafted. Tor Dahl told me, "They only draft you if you have exceptional skills."

Joffe told me that "70 percent of men and 30 percent of women get an 'invitation'" to join the military since they only want the fittest. He pointed out that the United States, as part of NATO, has started storing tanks, amphibious assault vehicles, armored Humvees, and missiles in caves in Norwegian mountains. "I don't know why. Maybe they are afraid of the Russians," Joffe said. "I think it's ridiculous that Americans come over and train in the snow in case of World War III. If that happens, none of Norway's money will help us."

All this talk of military preparation for a Russian invasion made the idea of the Nobel Peace Prize presented in Oslo a bit strange. This paradox of peace is evident in the brutal history of the Vikings while modern Norway has been the world leader in many peace accords.

Some wished that the Norwegians would just mind their own business and keep out of other countries' problems. In *Time* magazine, I read that Mangala Samaraweera, a friend of the president of Sri Lanka, complained to the media about Norway's meddling in their peace process with the Tamil Tigers. "Of course, we can't expect anything better from a nation of salmon eaters who have turned into international busybodies," he said.

When I told this quote to Inger, she was perplexed. "That's an insult? It seems more like a compliment. Salmon is very good."

Besides the Nobel Peace Prize, Norway's push for peace continues thanks to the Peace Research Institute Oslo, the Norwegian Initiative on Small Arms Transfers, and the

Norwegian Refugee Council, among other organizations. For a country with a population of just five million—slightly less than Minnesota—perhaps Norwegians truly are "international busybodies" for peace.

Amid all this controversy for peace and stability, I explained to Eilif that fifteen years ago I had the opportunity to see the Nobel Peace Prize ceremony here in Oslo.

Our friend Knut said, "I've seen it before."

"Oh, really? You've seen them give the peace prize?" I wondered.

"Well, I've seen it on TV, actually, just the highlights on the news. The whole ceremony is really too boring to watch, although being there is probably exciting."

I remembered when we lived in Trondheim that the Norwegian news ran it as the lead story for days, if not weeks. After all, this is Norway's moment in the sun.

I had gotten my hands on a ticket to that year's ceremony through the Fulbright Foundation but had to endure an eight-hour bus trip south over the mountains from Trondheim to Oslo to get there. At first, I took advantage of the free tea and instant coffee provided by the driver as I looked out the window at the stunning snow-covered peaks. The remaining hours, however, I jittered in my seat from the caffeine and fear as the driver wove around the icy switchbacks lined with two-foot-high guardrails to protect the double-decker bus from tumbling off a cliff. My only respite was the very frequent trips to the bus's tiny restroom from all that free tea. Inside, I felt my teeth chatter from the vibrating diesel engine underfoot, and I bounced from wall to wall with each turn as I tried diligently not to miss my mark.

I reminded myself that this excruciating bus ride was to see the king at the ceremony for the most important Norwegian award: the Nobel Peace Prize.

I thought of all the controversial Nobel prizes, especially those for literature awarded in Stockholm: Jean-Paul Sartre declined the award since he didn't want to "be transformed into an institution." When Norwegian writer Knut Hamsun won his Nobel prize, he sent the medal to Nazi propaganda chief Joseph Goebbels. I can brag that two Nobel prize-winners for literature hail from Minnesota, Sinclair Lewis and Bob Dylan, but strangely F. Scott Fitzgerald never won it.

That year, Iranian human rights lawyer Shirin Ebadi had won the prize and posed a challenge to the conservative mullahs in Iran. The committee hoped the prize would make her nearly "invulnerable" as she continued her struggle for the rights of women and children. Some journalists, however, criticized Ebadi as not being critical enough of the repressive Iranian government.

For the peace ceremony, held in December, a thick blanket of fog covered Oslo, and no light penetrated until after 10:00 a.m. This stark contrast to the heat of the Middle East didn't stop demonstrators in front of the Grand Hotel rallying to remind Shirin Ebadi to push for rights for Azerbaijanis and Kurds in Iran. "Stoning is a very cruel and barbaric act," stated placards—an argument difficult to dispute—while a cassette played Ravel's "Bolero" crescendos through a little Marshall amplifier.

Rainbow flags draped from windows around Oslo with the word "FRED!" emblazoned across the colors. I assumed Fred was a local politician, perhaps an incumbent in search of reelection. My trusty dictionary explained *fred* in one word: "peace."

In front of the Rådhus, four thousand children gathered waving little flags proclaiming *"Redd Barn"* (Save the Children). A group of kids—some wearing Santa Claus caps and other immigrant students covered with Islamic headscarves—played hide-and-seek while their teachers tried desperately to round them up.

Traffic was diverted for a block around the Rådhus by policemen whose guns were appropriately absent in honor of the peace prize ceremony. This low-key security stood in stark contrast to the U.S. Embassy's fence of razor wire and two sets of checkpoints to enter through metal detectors.

I asked the Norwegian guards at the Rådhus where the entrance was, but they looked me over unconvinced. I was wearing a suit that was wavy with wrinkles from the eight hours sleeping on the bus. "No, really, I have a ticket," I implored them. I proudly handed them my invitation, and one guard looked at it surprised.

"He really does have a ticket. Look!" he told his partner.

They examined the ticket closely, perhaps to make sure it wasn't a forgery, and grudgingly let me in the doors. I joked to them that this year I might really have a chance to win the prize.

"No, they've already decided the winner," the guard sneered humorlessly.

I watched the VIPs graciously enter the hall as though expecting a red carpet. Some men were shocked they had to wait in line to check their cashmere overcoats and their wives' oversized minks.

I knew no one here but tried to mingle with a group of politicians. One man looked at me and asked, ". . . and who are you?" I was saved by the bell as the time had come to take our seats for the ceremony.

Just as the thousand or so diplomats were ready to take their seats, Michael Douglas walked in with a beautiful young woman who must have been his daughter. The buzz rippled through the crowd that a movie star was here to promote peace.

"It's Catherine Zeta-Jones!" exclaimed the bejeweled woman next to me who was doused with entirely too much Chanel N°5. "Excuse me, I have to meet her!" She pushed me aside and nearly snagged her lengthy earrings on my wavy suit. She used her elbows and polite apologies to approach the movie stars.

A crowd gathered around Michael Douglas and Catherine Zeta-Jones, and the once stoic diplomats eagerly put out their hands or a slip of paper and pen for an autograph. The stars graciously obliged to sign a few programs and shook hands awkwardly stretched over the shoulders of those closest to the famous pair. The excited crowd grew as the famous pair was just trying to sit down because they had arrived late. This was the only time I'd seen Norwegians lose their cool.

I saw the woman who was sitting next to me walk right up and hold her camera a foot from the faces of the famous couple.

"PAFF!" The flash startled them. The movie stars blinked repeatedly to regain their eyesight, but more Norwegians' cameras were thrust into their faces. "POFF! PAFF!" Some of the starstruck politicians put their arms around the couple for this photo op, as the stars had no alternative but be embraced.

"PAFF! POOF!" the flashes sparkled as the blinded couple kept smiling for the lens. Finally, a guard came to relieve them from the flood of flashes. With the crowd dispersed, the stars reached for the back of their chairs to sit down without tumbling over.

I smelled the woman next to me coming back and felt her heel crunch my toes as she struggled back to her seat. On her camera, she proudly showed off her photo of Michael Douglas and Catherine Zeta-Jones, who were wide-eyed and frightened by a potential new stalker.

A woman behind us—wearing a turquoise sequined dress and a cup of Gucci cologne—was upset that the guards wouldn't let her take a photo as well. "I have absolutely no sympathy for stars when they're always complaining about getting no privacy and hounded by paparazzi," she said enviously. "That's the life they chose, and it's our money that made them what they are." She calmed down when my neighbor offered to send her a copy of her photo.

The conversation turned to speculative whispers when two regal guards rolled a red carpet down the aisle. Trumpeters stood at attention in the balcony and held their position for twenty minutes until after the Nobel committee and the prizewinner, Shirin Ebadi, walked the carpet to a standing ovation.

"BAA BAA BADA! BAA BAA BADA!" The royal heralds blasted through their bugles. An embroidered cloth dangled from the extended bell of their horns. Queen Sonja of Norway strutted in accompanied by her son, Crown Prince Haakon. The woman next to me offered color commentary by whispering, "It's only because the king is in hospital that Sonja's son can accompany her." After I'd endured a hellish eight-hour bus trip to see the king, he'd eluded me.

Even though I see no use for royalty, I do like that Norwegians voted to have a king and had to import him from Denmark. That king had married his cousin. Their son, and future king, also had married his cousin. The imported king only spoke Danish and never really learned Norwegian. The constitution, after all, was written in Danish, and until recently new amendments had to be in the old Danish style.

When I saw the royalty, I couldn't help but think of the gala held in 1648 for the coronation of the king of Denmark and Norway, Frederick III. The celebration for one thousand guests took place in three separate buildings to make room for the banquet. All the food from the local area—pigs, sheep, chickens, eggs—was confiscated for the feast, and nets scooped up nearly all the fish from the fjord. For toasts to the king, the guests smashed more than sixteen hundred glasses against the wall and then ripped the wallpaper off in a frenzy. Eight years later another party rivaled it with twelve courses with seventy-eight roast oxen and more than thirteen hundred chickens. At this second party, the guests shattered the windows and absconded with the drapes.

Modern times are a bit more modest, and the main decadence is royal hats. Prince Haakon's wife, Mette-Marit (a commoner and not his cousin), walked behind him wearing an enormous purple velvet hat. "Royalty always wear hats, you know," my neighbor said to her friend. Mette-Marit managed to avoid the pregnant woman waddle even though she was due in a month. Nearly constant flashes sparkled from the press cameras in the balcony because Mette-Marit was front-page fodder for the Norwegian tabloids, which speculated on the sex of her unborn baby.

The Norwegian Nobel Committee leader gave an extended speech with excerpts of Rumi poems as I struggled with my headset that provided translation from *nynorsk*, one of the three official languages of Norway, which fewer than 15 percent speak. The English channel erupted into static every couple of minutes, perhaps from interference from a passing plane, and a quarter of the audience pulled off their earphones from the deafening buzz.

Thankfully, some quiet piano music—from Norwegian composer Edvard Grieg, of course—calmed the crowd. Then a Persian group, the Kamkars, dispelled any formality by lighting up the hall with a wild and melodic folk song that reflected the excitement in the room for the peace prize.

With the backdrop of a three-story mural entitled *Work, Administration and Celebration* featuring stone-faced brick-layers raising their hands in victory, Shirin Ebadi accepted the peace prize from a man two heads taller than her. He lowered the microphone to her level, but when she spoke from the podium, she seemed like a giant. Her speech not only pushed for reform in Iran but condemned the United States for not abiding by all United Nations Security Council mandates. Although some argue she wasn't radical enough because she still embraced an Islamic government, she wore no headscarf. Her eleven books, her Defenders of Human Rights Center, and her children's rights organizations showed evidence of her conviction.

At the end of the ceremony, two cords were extended down the aisle to keep the audience in place while the royal family and their large hats made their exit to the sound of trumpets.

Soon after the royal cords were withdrawn, I saw the woman next to me get wrapped in her fur coat by her husband and whisked off to the formal Nobel reception at the Grand Hotel.

Before climbing on the bus for the eight-hour trip back to Trondheim, I saw the jubilant crowd gathered in front of the Grand Hotel late into the night to see the prizewinner greet them from her balcony before her return to Iran.

The next day on Norwegian newsstands, Zeta-Jones beat Ebadi for the cover photo because of the movie star's dazzling hairstyle change from earlier in the day and her dazed expression from all the flashbulbs.

Stranger Language

KATY AND I assumed Eilif would be a full-fledged Norwegian since he was born in Orkanger. We dreamed he'd be a dual citizen and could choose to attend school and work either in Norway or the United States and then have an open door to the rest of Europe thanks to the Schengen Agreement. Nope. We found out only after he was born that Norway doesn't offer birthright citizenship. Eilif would have to live in Norway for a few years before he could even apply for citizenship.

Denying birthright citizenship is what many anti-immigrant groups have been pushing in the United States, so I was surprised that Norway had long ago rejected this right. President Trump was privately overheard saying we needed fewer immigrants from "shithole" countries, and then, with the prime minister of Norway, Erna Solberg, at his side, he encouraged more Norwegians to immigrate to the United States. Solberg didn't know how to take this backhanded compliment. Strangely, Trump had a history of promoting Scandinavia since his biography claimed he was of Swedish ancestry, perhaps reckoning his German background would be unpopular. After Trump's invitation to Norwegians to move to the United States, my friends in Oslo saw little reason to give up Norway's great system and were generally embarrassed by the president's strange flattery.

Immigration is a thorny issue in Norway, as the country adapts to new arrivals. Jarle, the teacher from Oslo, remarked, "Suddenly there are too many foreigners, and our social system can't help everyone." I pointed out that I was one of these foreigners and took advantage of the system when we lived in Trondheim and Katy gave birth to Eilif. For some reason, that was all right, but I had a sneaking suspicion it was because I have Scandinavian ancestry.

"Norway is shrinking in native population and needs more people. That scares a lot of people," economist Tor Dahl told me. "Norway should try to get as many people to come in as possible for growth."

I talked to Anna, the third-year law student from Oslo studying in Minnesota, about how everyone living in Norway is entitled to the social services from the government. She didn't like my word choice. "Entitled? That's an interesting word," she replied. "Why should immigrants who just arrived in the country be 'entitled' to benefits when regular Norwegians who have been working their whole lives aren't?"

She thought that I saw Norway as too much of a democratic socialist utopia where poverty has been eliminated. "You were here in 2004, but things have changed," she said. "Now you see people on the streets of Oslo begging, and the poor are poorer."

I replied that since we left fifteen years ago, Norway was proclaimed the happiest country on earth. Anna went against the usual party line that I'd heard across Norway: "That's bullshit. No one is talking about the income difference in Norway. Everything is so expensive. The rich are getting richer, and the only ones who get anything from the government are new immigrants." While this was clearly an exaggeration, she wasn't alone in thinking that they shouldn't be so generous to newcomers. Oslo's residents are the second richest in the world with an average income of seventy-four thousand dollars. No wonder I couldn't afford anything here and worried that we barely had the funds for a good lunch.

Petter, the tour bus driver from Trondheim, complained to me that foreigners were snatching up Norwegian jobs and they couldn't stop them. "A Lithuanian, Latvian, or Estonian driver can bring in a group of Chinese tourists. They pay that driver for ten days what I make in two days. There are laws, but they falsify the documents. Soon we will have no more Norwegian bus drivers. Why would you want a driver who doesn't know the country and doesn't speak the language?"

As he told me this, we saw a German tour bus that had stopped because some of the cases of beer and schnapps they had smuggled in the trunk had sprung a leak. They didn't care they were breaking the laws with trafficked booze because they saved so much money by risking it.

Magne backed up Petter's point: "Soon all the foreigners will be doing the work and Norwegians will be *naver*," referring to the term used for being on the government dole. "Soon Norway will be just a big tourist area," Magne said and pointed out that giant cruise ships are even docking in Bodø.

As a tour guide, Magne teased many of the foreigners he met who were working in Norway by speaking only Norwegian to them. When they didn't understand, he switched to English and joked that he would check back in a year to see how good their Norwegian was.

Many critics of Scandinavian exceptionalism point out that it's much easier to have successful social welfare in such homogeneous countries, but in Oslo 25 percent of the population comes from other countries. Inger pointed out that her daughter's school in Oslo is very diverse: "In Ada's class, we started counting the different countries: Italian, Somali, American, Bosnian, English . . . there were fifteen different nations."

After Poland, Sweden supplies the most immigrants to Norway. Tor told me, "There's very little difference between the rich and poor in Norway in a company." Then he added a jab at Norway's neighbor, where the disparity between the lowest paid and highest paid employees has grown: "Sweden is worse."

To outsiders, the difference between Swedes and Norwegians may seem silly, but they don't see it that way—even if the two countries have often talked about forming a union again to streamline various services, such as the telephone companies, banking, and so forth. The problem is who would be in charge? A Norwegian or a Swede? Then what would happen if the Danes get involved? None of them dare give up their identity, or power over their future.

The Swedes tend to view the Norwegians as their rural cousins, almost hillbillies with too much money now because of all the offshore oil fields. My Swedish grandmother complained about her Norwegian in-laws, who were terrible housekeepers and couldn't keep their home clean.

A Swedish journalist who now lives in Washington told me, "I like the Norwegians, but they are just a little dull." The Swedes seem to consider themselves much more cosmopolitan—just look at the difference between the

Viking Ship Museum in Oslo and the regal Vasa Museum in Stockholm.

The Scandinavians brought this friendly animosity to the United States. Swedish American historian Amandus Johnson wrote about the ingrained stereotypes that the Danes only wanted to eat, the Swedes only wanted to sing, and the Norwegians only wanted to fight. Another one I heard more often was "Norwegians eat to live; Swedes live to eat; and the Danes eat to drink." Another attempt at categorizing them was by the editor of the *Metro Lutheran* newspaper, who told me how the different nationalities acted: "The Norwegians cause the most fuss, the Swedes rebut anything the Norwegians say, and the Germans just stay quiet."

I remembered our landlord in Trondheim, Arne, explaining that his grandfather came over the border from Sweden to settle near Bodø. "You're partially Swedish then?" I asked him.

He nodded quietly, almost embarrassed.

"That's OK," I said, and he laughed.

Sweden as well has had many immigrants, and Torstein, the Swedish German bus driver, told me, "Sweden pays some immigrants to go home for a visit." As in Norway, Sweden has tried to help these immigrants make a successful adjustment to their new country, but not without some resentment of Swedish taxpayers who foot the bill.

Divisions within Norway's own borders are vast considering it has 350 different spoken dialects and three official languages (*bokmål, nynorsk,* and Sami). How does anyone understand each other in this country of just over five million, especially when everyone rebels against the standard *bokmål,* saying, "Speak your dialect!"? The Bergen dialect has the French/German *r,* and the Trøndersk dialect of

Trondheim is practically unintelligible. Instead of saying *Jeg vet ikke* (I don't know), they say *A vet itj*. Many of the more obscure dialects have started to die out, and some Scandinavian scholars have traveled to the Midwest to study the Nordic enclaves where the last surviving speakers of those dialects live.

The Norwegian word for immigrants is *innvandrere*, which looks like "invaders" but is more like "in wanderers," as if they got lost somehow. The word for "foreign language" in Norwegian is *fremmedspråk*, which is more like "stranger language." The Norwegians I met, however, are remarkably nimble in switching from their dialect to *bokmål* to perfect English. They can understand Swedish perfectly, comprehend Danish well enough, and generally speak another European language as well. My friend Astrid told me, "Everyone, or at least most people, goes for a year in another country. It's rare to find someone who hasn't lived in, or at least traveled to, another country."

In general, Norwegians are remarkably well read and worldly for a remote northern country. They spend more on books per capita than anywhere else in the world. Norwegians are tied with Japan for the highest percentage of readers of daily newspapers. On average, each Norwegian spends an hour a day reading the newspaper. In Oslo, though, I just see people on their phones, possibly reading the digital editions.

On the train one day, some folks from the town of Asker told me, "We usually read the local newspaper, but they only report on events that happen to people from town. If there wasn't someone from Asker in the war in Afghanistan, we wouldn't even know that there was a war there! We have to read the national papers for that kind of news."

Even though I'd heard claims that people "subscribe to three or four newspapers," I couldn't help thinking that these "respectable" newspapers all look like scandal sheets, and almost all are tabloid sized. At the train station, the rack for *The Economist* had been replaced with a Norwegian newspaper that in bold black letters promised all the details of someone wanting to set a "*Gruppe-Sex*" record.

Despite this yellow journalism, the newspapers generally veered to the left, which reflected most of the population. In one of the classes I took in Trondheim, a fellow student asked me, "Why is it that in the United States there are two political parties that are to the right of all the parties in Norway?"

Overall, Norway has sought to level the playing field for everyone, especially women. Tor explained that, by law, women need to make up at least 40 percent of the governing boards of companies. "Norway has fewer strikes after women and workers have access to boards," Tor told me. He pointed out that women "dominate virtually all education and the university system. This gives them power and influence. We have found that women tend to be better leaders. They are much better communicators since men are basically mute until the age of eighteen!"

Good governance has made Norway a destination for immigrants in search of a better life, even if they have to forge official papers. Hans Erik said falsified documents are not so common with immigrants, but his wife, Anne, says it's very common and happens mostly from the Baltic countries.

I told them that I'd like Eilif to have the option to study here, but he doesn't have the documentation—just a clipping from the newspaper in Orkanger that announced his birth. Apparently, if Eilif learns Norwegian well enough and can afford living expenses, he can go to school in Norway tuition free as an immigrant. Maybe it's just fine that he's not a Norwegian citizen.

Environment

"I'VE SEEN MORE TESLAS in the past hour than I've seen in a year in Minnesota," Eilif said as we walked the streets of Oslo. More than 22 percent of cars in Oslo are hybrid or electric, and 56 percent of new car sales in Norway are for electric vehicles. I wondered, though, how anyone could afford these luxurious Teslas. Once again this is all due to the not so invisible hand of the government. To discourage use of the internal combustion engine, the Norwegian government has decreed that all new car sales must be electric by 2025. To get there, electric cars can use bus lanes, get free parking, have free recharging, and pay no tolls. These perks have been rolled back slightly, but in Oslo not paying tolls is impossible to resist since toll stations seem to pop up everywhere on major roads.

The biggest incentive, however, is taxes. Up until 2020, the Norwegian government required no tax on electric vehicles, but still the taxes are significantly less than for gas vehicles. I'd heard that the Danish government added an astounding 150 percent tax on full-size, gasoline-powered automobiles. "Oh, Norway is higher than that—except for electric cars," said Runa's friend who worked at Equinor, Norway's national oil and gas company.

I thought there was a mistake, considering the sticker

price for a new Volvo is, say, $60,000. With 150 percent tax, the total comes to $150,000. Kjell Bergh, who owns Borton Volvo in Golden Valley, Minnesota, confirmed that the tax, especially on the bigger vehicles, can be even higher in Norway. On top of that, gasoline costs nearly eight dollars per gallon, despite little Norway supplying the world with so much oil and natural gas.

I asked the woman who worked at Equinor if it's hypocritical of Norway to have a giant oil industry and claim to be environmentally friendly. "It's all the red parties that want to just stop drilling for oil and shut down the platforms, but we have to be practical," she told me. She worked out on the North Sea on the giant oil platforms, which are like little villages. To be permitted to go out to these platforms, she had to undergo helicopter training, which included a simulation exercise in which she had to escape from her seat belt while submerged and flipped upside down in a swimming pool. Despite how stable these oil platforms look, "you have to brace yourself because the waves constantly make it move," she said.

She considered herself an environmentalist but also a realist. "We have to carry two thoughts at once. We have to use our oil for good. All of Norway gets its energy from hydro. We have solar panels on the roof of our house, so we produce at least a quarter of our electricity." She told me that her husband often has to climb on the roof in the middle of winter to clear off the snow. "You should do the same in the United States rather than burning coal."

Equinor is now a publicly traded company on the New York Stock Exchange, she told me. Norway still owns 40 percent of the company but gets 75 percent of the profits, which are funneled into the enormous *oljefond,* or oil fund.

"That seems like a pretty good deal for Norway," I said.

"Of course it is."

I teased her that she now sounded like she was from one of those red parties advocating socialism and sharing the wealth.

"I suppose I am compared to your parties in America. All of this is possible thanks to democratic socialism."

She explained that Norwegians pressure each other to help save the environment. "A family came from Sri Lanka, and the father was a doctor," she told me. "He wanted a big, expensive Mercedes, but we convinced him to try a little electric car for a while. He soon realized that the electric car was plenty."

To fulfill Norwegians' stereotype about the United States, I explained that when the Drægni relatives visited us in Minneapolis I wanted them to experience "American Day" and spend as much time as possible in our cars. First thing in the morning, we stopped for drive-through coffee, then the drive-through bank, drive-through pharmacy, a drive-in diner for lunch, and finally, to top off the day, a drive-in theater. "The only time we left our car was to use the bathroom," I said.

They were horrified and didn't think it was funny at all. "You Americans just need to use less!" the woman from Equinor replied. "I lived with a family in South Bend, Indiana, and they were well-off so they just wasted so much. You can't do that. We try to reuse and conserve in Norway."

Both the government and people push for fewer cars on the road. I didn't know of any Norwegian family that had two cars since they used public transportation or got around by bike or foot. "We are encouraged to leave the car at home and use public transportation," Gro from Bergen told me and left out who was doing the encouraging. As the paranoid American, I was left to assume it was Big Brother.

The Norwegian government has proposed making all public transportation—especially in Oslo—completely free. Perhaps this was one reason the bus driver didn't make Eilif and me pay when I couldn't get the correct change. Compare this to when my mom got on a bus in Germany with my two brothers and me when we were little and didn't have the correct change. The driver called the police, who were going to arrest us until a nice man gave her the deutsche marks to avoid jail time.

I saw people using the tram and buses all the time, but the Minneapolis *Star Tribune* wrote, "In virtuous Sweden . . . people aren't driving much less or switching fast enough to fuel-efficient and electric cars." Cars in Sweden last an average of 9.9 years, which is lower than the European Union's 10.8 years. I noticed in Norway that all the cars are immaculate and had no signs of wear. In the United States, we drive the cars into the ground, which seems much more environmentally friendly. Norwegian friends mentioned that their cars needed to be "changed" every few years, even if they have just a little rust.

Petter, the bus driver from Trondheim, said, "You have to bring your car to the 'doctor' every two years," where they decide if it's roadworthy. He mentioned as well that drivers have to renew their license every year after age seventy-five. You have to have your doctor's permission to keep the car on the road. Bus drivers can't drive after seventy."

I'd heard people in Oslo complain that politicians want more and more toll stations to discourage driving. To meet demand for more public transportation, the city of Oslo just ordered two hundred new electric buses.

At present, Norway produces more electricity than it can use, mostly through hydropower. Economist Tor Dahl told me that "99 percent of renewable energy is Norway's contribution to global warming." He explained that Norway noticed early on the impending climate disaster: "Water in lakes got brown. Fish are moving north away from Lofoten to Russia."

"The Russians will like that," I responded. "More fish for them!"

Tor responded grimly, "They probably drink more than they eat."

The need for more power, though, has dotted Norway with giant windmills to supplement electricity from hydro. Some Norwegians have protested because windmills on mountains "destroy" the landscape.

Jan wants nuclear power. Otherwise, he told me, "Norway will have to cover 10 to 15 percent of its land with 250-meter-tall windmills or 10 percent of its sea with windmills."

He pointed out that although coal has a bad reputation, it saved the environment at one time. "Norway, and all of Europe for that matter, would have been completely deforested—just like Iceland—by the 1800s if it hadn't been for coal. We've gone from wood to coal to oil to electricity." I wasn't sure if he could convince his fellow Norwegians about nuclear power since most don't consider it environmentally friendly after Chernobyl.

Meanwhile, the city of Oslo has set a goal to cut emissions by 95 percent before 2030 and to be carbon-neutral by 2050. Because of this and other initiatives, Oslo was declared the "European Green Capital" in 2019.

I saw that Oslo even has a Recycling Festival in October for people to exchange or reuse items and give them "a new lease on life." To swap clothes and other used things, Oslo residents have set up "exchange markets" and sometimes even lend tools and offer courses on sewing or how to fix broken items. I read that Janne Gillgren, who works at Friends of the Earth Norway, said, "If all Norwegians exchanged three garments a year instead of buying new clothes, we could reduce CO_2 emissions by the same amount as if all car owners in Norway stopped using their vehicles for five days."

When Eilif and I returned back to our friends' house for dinner, their son, Henrik, was upset because the winners of a song contest at his school "only won because their song was about the environment." He thought that they were flattering the judges by just playing what they wanted. Eilif agreed that mixing politics and music is tricky. By the end of the conversation, though, Henrik had a new idea for the contest. He was enthusiastic about a song he'll enter into the contest next time that talks about saving the environment.

Volunteering

HANS ERIK SHOWED EILIF AND ME around the woods near their suburban apartment and pointed out the hilly park with a neighborhood "communal ski slope" where Henrik skied during the winter. Rather than a corporate ski area, this hill required parent volunteers to run the T-bar ski lift and concession stand. Anyone could come to ski, but they were expected to chip in and help out. I told him that this is a stark contrast to for-profit ski areas in the United States, which can be very expensive. If we lived here, Eilif would know how to downhill ski by now rather than just cross-country ski.

Hans Erik told about us about his sister, who decided to move back to Norway after twenty-five years in the United States and was struggling to fit back in. Hans Erik was confused about homeschooling in the United States, which isn't allowed in Norway. He wondered if homeschooling just divided people across America rather than bringing them together, since almost all children in Norway go to public schools. Only about 2.5 percent of Norwegian kids go to private K-12 schools, compared to 10 percent in the United States.

Teachers in Norwegian schools don't give grades until the eighth grade to downplay competition and build up self-confidence. Kari, the professor of education from Bergen, said making happy citizens all starts with the kids becoming a "complete human being" through the Norwegian education system, which integrates them into the culture. "Children are happy in school," she stressed and made a jab at the much-touted educational system in Finland, which has no homework and music everywhere: "Finnish children are among the lowest in terms of happiness," she claimed.

Jarle, the teacher in Oslo, thought that parents might be spoiling their kids: "There's a danger in becoming too content. You become too self-centered, so we try to teach kids to walk in each other's shoes in Norway." He'd found in his years of teaching that kids are now striving for perfection rather than being content with who they are. "A strange thing about kids now is they're trying to be *too* good," he told me. "They are too much into being the best kid in the class. It's too much. They are working too hard. They want to show off in too many fields. I have to tell some of my students not to do too much."

Tonja in Bergen had a similar situation: "My daughter wants to be a veterinarian, but she wants to study too much. I tell her that she doesn't need to be top of her class since many kids have so much stress and more mental problems. You just need to be good enough so you can be happy."

The tension between educating independent, self-reliant kids who are also happy depends on family and community support. This begins with *barnehage*, or preschool/kindergarten for children ages one to five. Most *barnehager* integrate "outdoor education," and, most important for many families, they are inexpensive and even free for some kids thanks to government subsidies.

Sissel, my Norwegian teacher in Trondheim, explained,

"There are so many important factors for happiness, but if I have to choose one, I would say the family politics, which have been such a success in Norway." She said that politicians finally have recognized that getting as many people employed as possible may be good, but more important is doing it in a way to not sacrifice friends and family. "I think a lot of countries forget how important women and mothers are to the economy—in Norway they are actually far more important than the oil! The key is to make working life manageable, especially for parents, to give generous parental leave and support childcare. We need to give people a chance to have a good balance between their working life and spare time. This give-and-take politics can make people happy."

Joffe told me that until the 1970s, the Norwegian government would send substitute housewives, *husmødre*, to help families in need. "When my mother was sick two times before I was fifteen, the government sent a *husmor* to our house to take over all the daily tasks. They were quite strict, but very professional." He told me that trying to keep everyone in Norway employed has not been good on kids. "Now that families are expected to have two parents working, it's been devastating on the home life. People are all rushing about, and all we do is work."

In Norway, 42 percent of marriages end in divorce (about the same as the United States), but Norwegian friends told me that there isn't the massive financial hit that often happens in America or the stigma attached to it. One small factor that helped nurture our marriage was the *dyne*, or single quilt, which saved our sleep since Katy and I each had our own covers and didn't have to fight for the comforter. The average marrying age of the typical Norwegian is older, with women averaging thirty-one years old and men at thirty-four, compared to twenty-seven and twenty-nine in the United States.

None of this takes into account *samboer,* or "cohabitants," who constitute almost a quarter of the population over age eighteen. Tor lamented, "With *samboer,* your door is sort of half-open. I think they're missing out." Even so, the Norwegian government recognizes the situation and gives automatic legal status to these civil unions.

I often didn't know if couples were married or *samboer,* and it didn't seem my place to pry. Some were "mixed families," or they used the much better term "bonus family," and both parents generally had equal custody after any divorce. As messy as relationships can be, I didn't witness much acrimony, or perhaps everyone was just very good at hiding any discontent.

At Hans Erik and Anne's house, Knut and Inger came over dinner, and we discussed Norway's standard of living and "happiness." Knut said, "In general, people here are pleased with their lives, but I think that perhaps we Norwegians have become a bit smug since we consider ourselves peaceful and helpful and a bit better than other places."

"I don't agree with you," Inger rebutted. "It's because we're all in this together. We have a willingness to give up part of ourselves for the whole."

I asked how she could pass on these ideas to their daughter, Ada, when teenagers seem so self-absorbed. Fortunately, Eilif didn't hear since he was playing guitar.

"We have very strict rules of how to raise a child, and we abide by the rules, but no one should tell us them! Swedes won't walk cross the road on a red light at 4:00 a.m., but Norwegians will!"

"You have to know about *dugnad*," Knut told me cryptically. This Old Norse word essentially means "communal work." "All neighbors chip in and help because you never know when you'll need the help."

I had noticed the flyer posted on Hans Erik and Anne's refrigerator with the word "DUGNAD! . . . We have the opportunity to volunteer," as if everyone was begging for an opportunity to chip in. I remembered all the school bake sales and fundraisers back home for our kids' schools.

I'd heard this word before in Trondheim when the woman who worked at Equinor told me that "all our children are coming back to paint the *hytte*. How do you say *dugnad* in English? It's our volunteering so we all work together."

"Oh, we would say it's the 'work weekend at the cabin,'" I said, "but our kids complain that it's 'slave labor.'"

Knut complained that the demands for *dugnad* are constant. "The new fundraiser is selling toilet paper."

"Everyone needs toilet paper, so they figured it was perfect," Inger added.

I was amazed: "You really have to sell toilet paper to your friends?"

"Yes, and now we have eighty rolls of toilet paper in our house waiting to be sold," Knut said. "Do you want to bring some Norwegian toilet paper back to Minnesota?"

Anne explained, "A father of a child at our school wanted to get out of *dugnad* and just asked how much he needed to pay to not have to do this, but you can't do that! Everyone has to volunteer."

"Nope, otherwise, we'd all do that to get out of it," Knut said.

"Well," Inger said, "he could just buy all the toilet paper

that he'll use eventually—but then he'd need an extra closet to store all the toilet paper!"

Anne said, "*Dugnad* is all about the community it creates."

Knut responded, "Yes, through toilet paper."

Takk for alt

Thanks for Everything

WHEN KATY AND I had moved to Norway fifteen years ago, Norwegians asked about our ancestry. I told them that my great-grandfather had come from the Sognefjord 110 years ago.

"You are welcome back!" they replied.

I didn't understand this, since I had never lived there.

Now, however, Eilif has returned to Norway and considers himself "Norwegian" since he was born in Orkanger. A few months after we left Oslo, Norway voted to allow dual citizenship.

Who knows what Eilif will do and where he'll be happiest. Whenever I asked Norwegians why they were so darn happy, I liked that their answers began with "we" rather than "I." While many people base happiness on how they are doing compared to others, Norwegians seem to want everyone to do well. It must be noted, however, that their numerous Olympic medals show that competition is alive and well.

Gro in Bergen replied, "I don't know if everyone is happy, but I am. But someone will always complain because they want more. We have very high taxes, but we have free hospitals. I only pay a little bit, really nothing, to go to the doctor. We have free university, and we are all taken care of when we get older. We are secure."

I wondered then if security is synonymous with happiness? Petter from Trondheim proclaimed, "If you are *lykkelig* you have everything you need and are happy." I had to question this whole idea of the "happiness scale" from the World Happiness Report when it rated El Salvador far above Italy in its ratings.

My teacher in Trondheim, Sissel, wasn't sure either: "I'm not totally sure what makes us so happy, but I know that the oil is not the main reason. The most important 'value' we have is the workforce, and I think most people pay their taxes and fees with pleasure knowing that they get so much back: free school and education, free hospital treatment, generous parental leave, etcetera. The safety you have if you lose your job or if you get ill is also priceless."

Many in the United States say that Norway can afford to provide all these social services because of all the oil money, but these systems are actually paid for by high taxes, especially income tax. The rich in these countries are highly taxed, making income equality not such a stark issue. Sweden and all the other Nordic countries have essentially the same system, which is one of the main reasons so many modern immigrants venture north.

I heard many Norwegians refer to their system as "democratic socialism" with a free market economy, since they said that the "democratic capitalism" of the United States essentially contradicts itself with the wealthy capitalists having more rights than the "democracy," or the people.

When I considered if this Norwegian model would work to help make the United States "happier," Jarle from Oslo responded, "I don't know if our system would work in America since Scandinavians, with Finland and Iceland, are only about 25 million people compared to 330 million in

the United States. Maybe one state—perhaps Minnesota?—could do it!"

My relatives left Scandinavia because of the abject poverty, but now Norway has one of the highest standards of living. Several years after we left Norway the prime minister even told his people to stop complaining that they didn't have enough things since they have one of the highest standards of living in the world.

The gross national income in Norway has tripled since 1992, which means Norwegian incomes generally have as well. Perhaps we should have found a way to stay after Eilif was born. Historian Odd Lovoll brought me back to earth: "No, you wouldn't have had the same opportunities in Norway. There are definitely more opportunities in the United States. For example, you wouldn't have a house if you had stayed in Norway."

Odd added, "I was in Oslo in February doing some research a few years ago and was just miserable." I told him that I remembered our experience during the winter *mørketid*, or dark time, in Trondheim and how I vowed never to experience that again. Showing Norway in May to Eilif is perhaps deceiving because of the glorious sunshine and good cheer with all the festivals.

Traveling with Eilif, I wanted him to really appreciate what we were seeing, but he seemed distracted. Then I remembered that when I was sixteen and in Scandinavia with my dad, I slept any chance I could get as we passed by pastoral scenes in Sweden, Hamlet's castle in Denmark, and the rugged, rocky shores of Norway. I do remember the delicious cookies, though. I think of that as Eilif devours cinnamon rolls and then takes a nap.

Even if my dad thought at the time that I didn't appreciate Scandinavia, apparently his efforts paid off because I brought Eilif on this voyage. I wonder how Eilif will look back on our trip. Who knows what journey he'll take and if he'll return to Norway someday, perhaps even with his own children. As we left, I told Eilif, "Thanks for everything"—or as Norwegians say when they leave: *Takk for alt!*

Glossary

Norwegian Words to (Maybe) Live By

allemannsretten: everyone's right to roam free over private property

arbeidsglede: work happiness

aske: ashes

babysvømming: baby swimming

barnehage: preschool/kindergarten for kids up to age five.

barnetog: children's parade during the *syttende mai* festival

berserkergang: blind rage

bokmål: standard Norwegian based on Danish (literally, "book language")

boligsamvirke: housing cooperatives

bryggen: the wharf

bunad: national costume that varies from region to region and worn for special occasions

dugnad: community volunteering

dyne: single quilt

døgn: twenty-four hours of daylight that happens in the north from May through August

elgskrekk: moose terror

fint som snus: fine as snuff

flink: clever

flyskam: flight shame

folkehøgskole: folk high school

folketrygden: the people's insurance

fram: forward

fred: peace

fremmedspråk: foreign language (literally, "stranger language")

fri oppdragelse: free upbringing for children

friluftsliv: outdoor life (literally, "free-air life")

frisk som en fisk: fresh as a fish

gammelungkar: old bachelor

gladelig: gladly

Gratuler med dagen!: Congratulations on the day!

grøt: porridge

Gullbrød: brand of Nidar dark chocolate–covered marzipan (literally, "gold bread")

heldig: lucky

helgefylla: weekend drinking binge

helvete: hell

hems: loft of a cabin

huldra: wood nymph; beautiful women who live in the mountains but have long tails, so are clearly not human

husmenn: tenant farmers

husmor: housewife, especially a substitute housewife used to help families in need

hvalburgere: whaleburgers

hygge: overused Danish word (which actually comes from Old Norse) meaning cozy and snug

hytte: mountain hut or cabin

høyre: right

ingefærøl: ginger ale

inneklimat: indoor air (literally, "inside climate")

innenfor ramen: "in the frame," or following the rules when renovating a house

innvandrere: immigrants (but looks like "invaders" and is literally "in wanderers")

iskrem: ice cream

Janteloven: Jante's Law, from a book that describes how everyone must conform and not think too much of themselves

Jeg vet ikke: "I don't know" (in Trøndersk, *A vet itj*)

jordnær: earthy (literally, "earth near")

kose seg: make oneself comfortable

koselig: cozy

kriminallitteratur: crime novels

kulturhuset: the culture house, or community center

landlig: country cozy

loppemarked: flea market

lusekofte: Norwegian sweater (literally, "lice sweater")

Lykke til!: Good luck!

lykkelig: happy

lystid: light time during the summer months

Lånekassen: Norwegian State Educational Loan Fund

matpakke: a packed lunch (literally, "food pack")

midnattsol: midnight sun

miljø: environment

myggnett: mosquito netting (literally, "bug nets")

mørketid: dark time in winter

naken: naked

nasjonalromantikken: the "national romantic" movement

naver: living on the government dole (based on the acronym NAV, Nye Arbeids og Velferdsetaten)

nisser: house pixies (Santa Claus is one of these)

nynorsk: "New Norwegian" that is a compilation of dialects and one of the official languages of Norway

nyttårsaften: New Year's Eve
nyttårsdag: New Year's Day
oljefondet: the oil fund
penger: money
polarnatt: polar night that can last from November through February
poser: bags
pulk: baby sled with rigid poles pulled by a cross-country skier
pygge: studs on tires
pølser: hot dogs
påskekyllingen: the Easter chicken
påskemarsipan: Easter marzipan
rupe: rope-like tassel that the *russ* strive to earn by doing pranks
russ: redhats, or graduating seniors in high school that undergo elaborate hazing rituals
russefeiring: weeks-long graduation celebration of the *russ*
russetog: *russ* parade during the *syttende mai* parade
rømmegrøt: cream porridge
saft: fruit juice
sakte: slow
Sakte By: "Slow City"
samboer: cohabitants in a civil marriage
selklubbing: seal clubbing
sikker: safe
sjø: sea
skadefryd: schadenfreude
skikjøring: skijoring, or skiing by being pulled, usually by a dog
slaps: snow and ice together, slush
Slik har de det der: literally, "That's how they got it there" (but means "That's different")

sludd: sleet
smørbrød: sandwich (literally, "butter bread")
snus: snuff
snøflugg: snowflake
sodd: meatball soup, a specialty of Trondheim
sol: sun
spark: kick-sled
spikertelt: temporary cabin (literally, "nails tent")
sprit: spirits, liquor
stavkirker: stave churches
sterk: strong
stjernehimmelen: the starry sky (or heavens)
svartmetall: black metal
Syden: the South (synonymous with vacation in the Mediterranean)
syttende mai: seventeenth of May, a national holiday for the signing of the constitution
Takk for alt: Thanks for everything
tran: cod liver oil
trikk: tram
trilling: walking with a baby stroller
trivelig: thriving
trygdekontor: insurance office
tunnelfeber: tunnel fever
Ut på tur, aldri sur: Out on a walk, never cross
velferdsstaten: the welfare state
Vinmonopolet: municipal liquor stores (literally, "The Wine Monopoly")
voksenpoeng: "adult points" earned by kids when they make grown-up choices
vårdepresjon: spring depression

Acknowledgments

To Jan Brøgger; Inger Brøgger, Knut Bull, and Ada Bull; Tor and Tove Dahl; Vigdis Devik; Magne, Rigmor, Lise, and Ole Magnus Drægni; Eilif Dregni for being a guinea pig; my dad for bringing me to Scandinavia as a distracted teenager; Magne Hatlevik; Petter Hovin; Katy McCarthy for her patience with all this Norwegianness; Jarle Nesvaag; Sissel Vuttudal Robbins; Astrid Solberg; Joffe Urnes and Runa Das; and Anne and Hans Erik in Ljan.

A warm *takk* to the University of Minnesota Press, especially Erik Anderson, Kristian Tvedten, and Heather Skinner, who encouraged me on my quest to discover what it means to be "Norwegian."

I am grateful to the Quasi Endowment Fund at Concordia University, Torske Klubben, and the Concordia Language Villages (especially Skogfjorden) for their support.

Eric Dregni is the author of twenty books, including *Vikings in the Attic* (Minnesota, 2011), *Weird Minnesota*, and *Let's Go Fishing!* (Minnesota, 2016). As a Fulbright fellow to Norway, he survived a dinner of *rakfisk* (fermented fish) thanks to 80-proof aquavit, took the "meat bus" to Sweden for cheap salami with a crowd of knitting pensioners, and compiled his stories as *In Cod We Trust: Living the Norwegian Dream* (Minnesota, 2008). He wrote about living in Modena, Italy, in *Never Trust a Thin Cook and Other Lessons from Italy's Culinary Capital* (Minnesota, 2009). He is director of the Italian Concordia Language Village during the summer and wrote about this experience in *You're Sending Me Where? Dispatches from Summer Camp* (Minnesota, 2017). He is a professor of English, journalism, and Italian at Concordia University in St. Paul, Minnesota, and he lives in Minneapolis with his wife, Katy, and three busy kids.